Best whs

George Lillywhite

A Tickle to Leg

The History of Upton-by-Southwell
and its Cricketers,
1855-1901.

by
George Lillywhite

MOORLEY'S Print & Publishing

© Copyright 1996 George Lillywhite

All rights reserved. No part of this publication may be
reproduced, stored in a retrieval system, or
transmitted, in any form or by any means,
electronic, mechanical, photocopying, recording
or otherwise, without the prior
written permission of the Publisher.

Commissioned publication

MOORLEY'S Print & Publishing
23 Park Rd., Ilkeston, Derbys DE7 5DA
Tel/Fax: (0115) 932 0643

CONTENTS

Chapter one
    A New Vicar Arrives — 9

Chapter two
    The First Match — 19

Chapter three
    Sympathy, Science, Strictures, and Libraries.
    The Work of Churchmen and Landowners — 26

Chapter four
    The Harsher Side of Life — 36

Chapter five
    Cricket in the Sixties' and Seventies — 44

Chapter six
    A School to be Proud of — 49

Chapter seven
    Nineteen Terrible Years — 52

Chapter eight
    Jubilees and Fun — 55

Chapter nine
    Upton's Golden Age — 60

Chapter ten
    Emigration — 67

Chapter eleven
    The End of a Reign — 72

Appendix A.	Bibliography.	76
Appendix B.	Victorian players and officials and years of membership. 1855-1901	77
Appendix C.	Matches played 1855-1901	80
Appendix D.	The first settlements in Upton, 600-800 AD	82
Appendix E.	The restoration of "The Old Vicarage"	84
Appendix F.	A feat of strength	86
Appendix G.	The "Daddy Upton" photographs	88

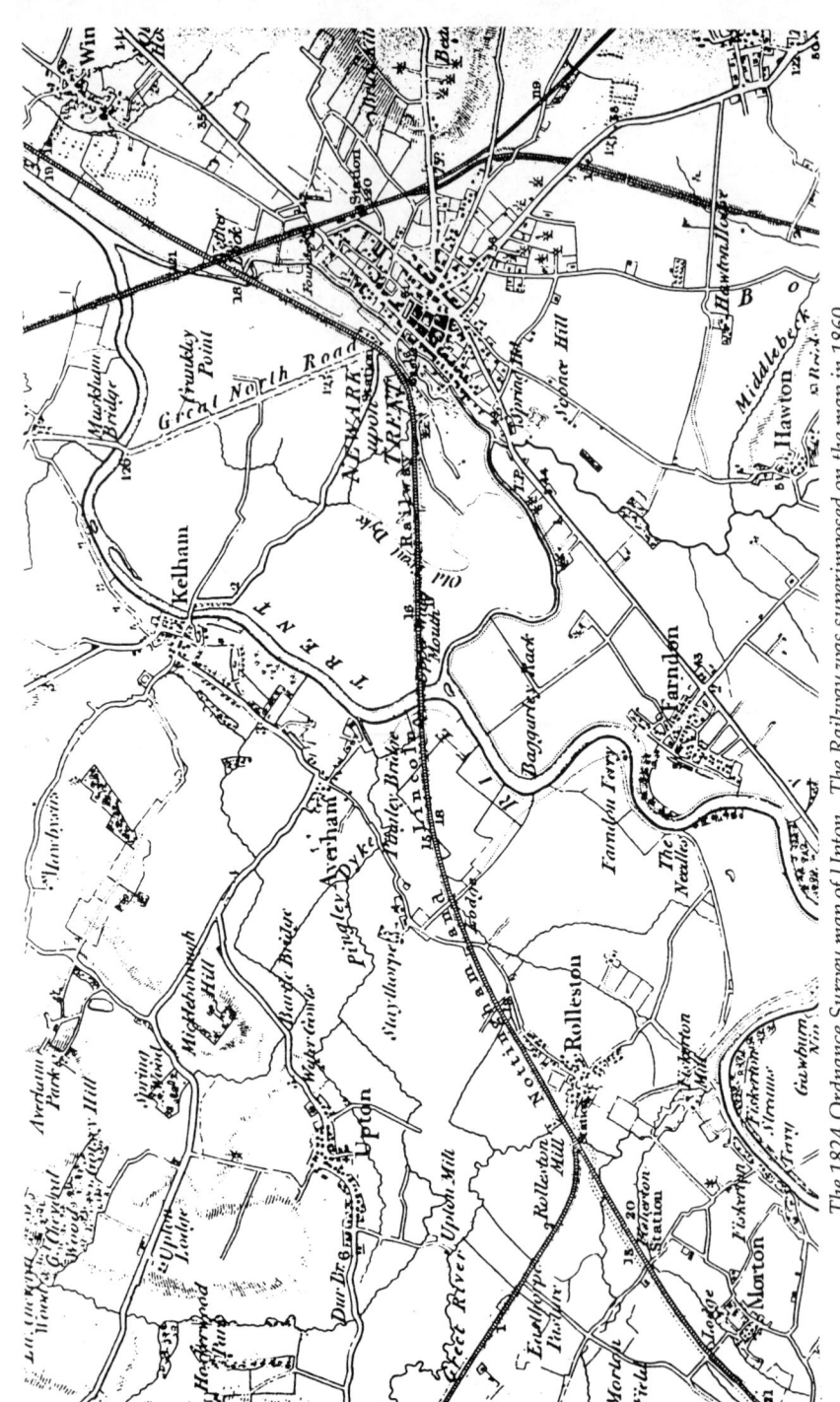

The 1824 Ordnance Survey map of Upton. The Railway was superimposed on the map in 1860.

Preface

The village of Upton has a population of about 500. Nearly a mile long, mostly of red bricks and pantiles, it stretches on each side of the A612 between Southwell and Newark in Nottinghamshire. Most of its one hundred and fifty homes are only a few feet from its main street; some are on the Trent's flood plain, others on rising ground nearer the church. The centuries have been kind; it is as unspoilt and attractive as a working village can be, with an ambience of space and shade at its centre, where Upton Hall stands among lawns and and fully grown trees.

One history of Upton has already been written. In 1947 the vicar, the Reverend Frank West, Archdeacon of Newark, 1947-1962, later Suffragan Bishop of Taunton, suffered a period of enforced idleness in "The Old Vicarage" just after his appointment. He was surrounded by snowdrifts, which later became floods, and also handicapped by power-cuts and fuel shortages. That winter is strongly backed to be the worst of the century. Virtually imprisoned, and looking for some useful task, he found the records of the churchwardens day-to-day transactions in a tin box in his vestry. He did what he could to draughtproof his study and, wrapped in a blanket, with a cocoa tin and a kettle at hand, began to work through the years, taking especial interest in those between 1600 and 1666. His careful selection of material, learned comments, and research eventually resulted in a series of talks to parishioners, then a fascinating history of Upton and its church from the last years of Elizabeth until the Restoration. Its title is "Rude Forefathers", taken from Thomas Gray's well-loved Georgian poem, "Elegy in a Country Churchyard", a thoughtful, sensitive and sympathetic appraisal of the farmworker of 1769; but this poem is far greater than the sum of its parts, and many think it the best poem in our language. It was conceived in the churchyard at Stoke Poges in Buckinghamshire, and therefore in a number of ways was suitable as the title of Frank West's book. The book is especially interesting to the parishioners of Upton for the description it gives of at least two recognisable houses, of the occupations of the villagers, its glimpses of the astonishing variety of people who passed through Upton, the village poor, the problems caused by the English Civil War, and the churchwardens' endless difficulties in relieving poverty and want with the limited resources at their disposal. After such erudition, should one of the village's cricketers choose to write another history? The answer is that a question was begged. What happened during the other thousand years?

This book probably began in the conversations between myself as fixtures secretary and David Ashworth, the chief groundsman, opening batsman, past-captain, chairman, and longest-playing member of the club. These usually took place against the south-east end of the bar in the "Cross Keys". As fixtures secretary I felt that it was my job to present an interesting list to the players every year; this meant looking for new fixtures. I had long coveted a friendly fixture against a Nottinghamshire XI, or even an MCC XI, but I knew there was little chance of securing one of these unless I could point to a significant anniversary. The thing to look for was our centenary year, and here the discussion became speculative and unsatisfactory. No-one seemed to have any idea at all when the club had played its first match. Only Ron Trueman, our former chairman, who had died in 1988, had seemed to have any idea. We had often heard him say,"My father played for Upton". Ron's father, Frederick Henry ("Harry") Trueman, was born in 1874 and died in 1966; this suggested that he could have played as a thirteen-year-old in 1887. The earliest factual evidence I had was an old minute book. It was a faithful record of twenty-eight years of committee meetings and social evenings, and yielded an astonishing amount of local history. A useful book could have been written from the information it provided about life in Upton in the second world war, and the decades that preceded and followed it. But there was no solid evidence of a cricket team before 1929. That meant the club was barely sixty years old - a long way short of its hundredth birthday.

When I asked David if I might have a look in the "old scorebooks" for clues, he replied he only had a few, but that Ron might have kept all the others. So I asked Mike Trueman, Ron's son, if I might see them. He had moved into High Farm after his mother had died. He promised to look for them, and said he had a lot of sorting out to do. There the matter was left to rest, and once again the seasons went by, and the pavilion had to be painted and new windows inserted. In the winter of 1992 we cut down a hedge along the south side of the ground and planted some trees. In the winter of 1993 I bought a mattock and took out or burnt all the remaining hawthorn stumps, so that a smooth curving bank could be easily flymoed.

A surprise came in December, 1994. Mike found the scorebooks, and brought them to me on a cold evening. There were 18, covering 29 seasons between 1929 and 1979, including all those from 1970-9. I was busy just before Christmas, so they had to lie in a cupboard until after Twelfth Night. I was certain that David Ashworth, who was in Australia for three months to watch some test matches, would have all the scorebooks from 1980 to the present day. That meant that every ball bowled and every run made in the last twenty-five years would be available for study. However, the first glances at the oldest book confirmed my deductions from the committee minutes; it was an established club in prosperous middle age rather than infancy. But, with this knowledge in hand, it was time to turn to the long established residents of the village to see if they could help the search back towards the earlier years of the century. Who was this man? Did his father play, or did he have older brothers? I discovered a firm consensus that a club existed during the Great War, but no-one had a shred of evidence to support this, not even the name of one player, except Harry Trueman.

It seemed than that the last hope was to telephone the secretaries of our opponents of 1929, and ask them whether we could look at their records. But here was another disappointment; not one of them had any scorebooks that dated back beyond the 1970's. The more distinguished the club, the more likely it was to have hurled everything into a dustbin quite recently. In fact they were deeply envious of our old scorebooks and the minute book, which seemed to become increasingly valuable with each phone call that I made. Here, in the middle of frustration, I decided to write some kind of history of Upton Cricket Club, if only to preserve the small body of evidence that was left to us. No other local club was in a position to do so; ours, if it could be written, would shed some light on theirs. So I was forced to assume that our club had started in the 'twenties, and started work with what I had, assuming we first played in 1929. I wrote twelve pages in the first week. Then the jigsaw altered; the club "aged" twice almost within hours; a final search started; the founder appeared; and finally, triumphantly and incontrovertibly, the date of origin.

Mike Trueman caused this hiatus. He telephoned me again late in January to say that he had made a further find in the back of a cupboard; a number of fixture cards. They were all embossed "Upton Cricket Club" in gold leaf, and the oldest was dated 1903. This was great news, and I went to look at them immediately. Yet the oldest card indicated, yet again, an established club; there was an authority about its officials, organisation, and rules which pointed firmly back to the nineteenth century; and if one can judge from the quality of a fixture card, which put our modern ones to shame, the club was not short of money, either. To my delight, I was looking from the Golden Age of cricket (1900-1914) back into the years when W.G. Grace first picked up a bat. I knew how Cortez felt, silent upon a peak in Darien, looking at the Pacific Ocean.

The next day I phoned Peter Wynne-Thomas, the author of many books about that era, and this was the crucial call, for it gained me generous professional assistance. Peter is also the president of the society of cricket statisticians, and the Nottinghamshire Cricket Club's archivist. He promised to look through his notebooks for me and phone back. Within a day he had, to say that he had found a report in the "Newark Advertiser", with full scores, of Upton playing Averham on July 30th, 1862. We were nearly back to the Crimean War. So I phoned Tim Warner, a historian and librarian in Newark, to ask whether I could search back through these early copies on the "Newark Advertiser" for match reports. He replied that the Advertiser had only started publication in 1859, but I certainly could; in the meantime, why didn't I phone the Nottinghamshire County Archives in Meadow Lane?

I did. It only took them quarter of an hour to find two small pieces of paper. One was a dated letter explaining why the club was being founded, and the other a printed prospectus with its rules and officers.

About ten years curiosity was completed satisfied, and I knew that the Upton Cricket Club was just three months short of its 140th anniversary. We could start planning 150th anniversary celebrations for 2005A.D. Furthermore, I had discovered that we were older than every other local club except two - Newark and Southwell. Finally, I was in a position to follow the example of my ancestor Fred Lillywhite and write yet another book about cricket; I had scorebooks, fixture cards, minute books, press cuttings, and a small host of people who "long remembered back". In fact, I soon had too much. While I found plenty of cricket matches to write about, I also found fascinating glimpses of village life; glimpses of strong characters and their attitudes, their triumphs, and their tragedies. Incidents began to knit together, and characters began to interact, as the microfilm rolled on. It would have been a crime to abandon what I found to dusty obscurity again, but one cannot spend one's life writing one book about a Nottinghamshire village. For the sake of brevity I had to limit it to the years of Victoria's reign.

My book is by an ordinary player about an ordinary club. Strangely, it grew until it was eleven chapters long. If I may quote John Arlott, *'It may contain team and individual successes; above all, though, it can evoke nostalgic memories, recall the heroes of forgotten generations, and provide a record of the happiness the game gave. A cricket club is a nucleus such as no other sport possesses in comparable numbers; a boy may grow up in its shadow, to play in his man hood, and watch in his old age a continuity he could hardly expect of other games. That, surely, is why cricket histories abound, and it will be a sad day for cricket when they cease to be written.'*

There are many people who gave me their time and help, and some have been mentioned already. It would be wrong to add further names now, for fear that I should offend some that I have temporarily forgotten. But anyone who is interested in Upton's history will find themselves knocking at the Story's door sooner rather than later, and to George and Violet my thanks are due for their humour and patience; and to Charles Beaumont, Stewart Deeman, Don Haxby, David Jordan, Kevin Templeman and Chris Weaver for their generosity. And to Helen Wood who read the proofs. Finally, my wife Christine's grasp of computer technology was decisive.

Chapter One
A New Vicar Arrives

It is not often that a cricket club knows with complete certainty the name of its founder. Upton can point with total confidence to a name on the list of vicars in its vestry. The Reverend Frederick William Naylor, B.A., aged 30, arrived in the vicarage in 1840. He succeeded the Reverend Thomas Still Basnett, who had not been required to live in the village, but probably lived in Southwell, riding out to Upton on Sundays to take services. The vicarage had probably been built in Tudor times or earlier. A seven roomed timber-framed building, it stood at a right angle to Church Lane where the north part of the present building stands. If one stands at the churchyard gate facing the vicarage, it stood in the position of the gable to the left of the front door. It had been let for centuries and fallen into disrepair. The church decided in 1840 that it should be rebuilt in brick for its new incumbent as had been the treatment for many of the village's houses and farmhouses since the turn of the century. It was also decided to add a completely new south wing of the house, to make room for the activities of a Victorian ministry, and more rooms to the north. So the dynamic young vicar found himself in a magnificent new rectory, with a large stone flagged hallway, three well proportioned reception rooms, and eight or nine bedrooms, standing at the top of the valley slope next to the church, facing southwards, with magnificent views across the Trent Valley to Belvoir Castle. The vicarage was not to know any further restoration until the 1970's, when after another period of abandonment following the removal of the Reverend West to Taunton, semi-dereliction once again occurred. The Reverend West recalled that when he had part of the rotting kitchen floor removed, where it had been customary to leave his children in their pram, a deep well was discovered. However, the village's finest and most well documented historic building was eventually saved from ruin by Lt. Cmdr Toomey and his wife Mary, who were looking for a home after moving from Northern Ireland (see appendix E).

Within a few years of the Reverend Naylor's arrival, gazing out at that view, he may well have picked out, not a mile away, men with flags marking a straight line across the flat meadows and dykes. If he did so, he would certainly have known them for railway surveyors, for he had arrived as the railway boom was gathering momentum. 2,400 miles of track had been laid by 1840, connecting London with Birmingham, Manchester, and Brighton. The Trent Valley Line was completed by

1846. Exactly one mile from his vicarage would be Rolleston station. In 1848 his parishioners would be able to travel as far as London or Glasgow, Holyhead or Dover. The days of the stagecoach were finished, and the age of cheap travel had arrived; in 1851 they would take advantage of cheap excursions to visit the Great Exhibition in Hyde Park, which celebrated England's industrial pre-eminence and ascendancy in the market place of the world.

In the meanwhile, Reverend Naylor looked out on a prosperous farming village. Agriculture in England in 1840 was at least two and a half times more efficient than in France, which was itself ahead of its European partners. This carried the momentum of the Industrial Revolution by making it possible to feed a population increasingly moving to industrial towns to work. Upton's farmland had been enclosed in 1795 and in 1861 there were about fifteen farms, the largest employing five men and a boy and covering 280 acres. But not all village employment was directly in agriculture. The Trade Directory lists 10 gentry and 42 traders including a baker, a biggler, blacksmiths, brick and tilemakers, cattledealers, graziers, joiners, millers, publicans, a schoolmaster, schoolteachers, shoemakers, tailors and wheelwrights, as well as farmers and yeomen. Furthermore, the 509 parishioners had other choices available in their working lives. Away from the village, they could work in Southwell or Newark, or they could move to Nottinghamshire or Derbyshire to work in textiles - Cromford, one of the springboards of the industrial revolution, is scarcely thirty miles from Upton - or they could emigrate to Australia or America. The image we should have of the working man of the 1840's is based on the army of a quarter of a million navvies who built the railways, fuelled by beef and beer, and then ran up the Crystal Palace in six months. The Reverend would also have seen at least three small schools in his parish. The old school was not built until 1864, but there was a dame school, his own Sunday school, and probably a Wesleyan Sunday school, for the Wesleyan chapel had been built in 1831. Two miles away in Southwell at least two more schools were available. The National School, which would later join with the Methodist Primary school to become Lowes Wong Junior School, was founded by an act of parliament in 1811, and the long established grammar school in the grounds of the Minster, now the Minster Comprehensive.

But all was not well in his parish; or, he might have said, not good enough. Some idea of the superstition and ignorance which gripped and limited the rural population can be gained from an incident in the very hard winter of 1854 to 1855. After a heavy fall of snow one morning it was noticed that right across England there were strange footprints in the snow across the gardens of cottages and up and over their thatched roofs. The rational explanation was that they were the clawprints or pawprints of cats and badgers and starlings and similar creatures, distorted and enlarged as the thaw set in. But no; the fact that they were in the gardens and on the roofs meant that the creature that made them had walked up the sides of the cottages, across the roofs, and down again, and it was not long before the tale gained credence that the devil had walked across England in a single night, a tale which persists to this day.

Some of the other problems and attitudes which the young and determined Reverend Naylor had faced in his ministry can be gleaned from this extract from the Newark Advertiser of February 29th, 1859, under "Local Intelligence".

'UPTON. - Child burnt to death. - On Monday about three o'clock, a woman named Stendall, wife of John Stendall, labourer, of Upton brickyard, went from her home for the purposes of visiting a neighbour, and left two children, one five years of age, the other four, in the house by themselves. In her absence the younger, Elizabeth Stendall, got some lucifer matches to play with, and in endeavouring to strike one alighted her pinafore, at least this is the version of the accident given by her elder brother. The poor child was most fearfully burnt before any assistance arrived, and when Mr. Calvert, surgeon, was sent for he declared nothing would save the child's life. Late in the evening the little sufferer expired from the injuries received. An inquest was held at the house of the parents, on Tuesday morning last, and after several witnesses had been examined the jury returned a verdict of "accidental death". The coroner (Mr. Newton) most strongly animadverted on the carelessness of the mother in leaving the children alone in the house, which strictures, however, the mother received, we regret to state, with perfect carelessness.'

This is the first mention of Upton in the "Newark Advertiser". Incidents of this kind would have depressed the vicar. We shall see that he was very unhappy about such low moral standards; we shall also see that he was the sort of man who would try to raise them - his work in the parish, his innovation would be simply that. He must have been driven by the irresistible urges and moral imperatives by which innovation was measured in the middle of the nineteenth century. Did a new idea elevate? Did it improve? Bribery, unbelief, drinking, wenching, gambling were gradually being regarded as archaic in these early years of Victoria's reign; progress and the rule of law were not inevitable but had to be fought for. One of the other causes of his uneasiness is obvious when we read the following letter, one of a number written on or about Wednesday the 25th of April, 1855. Only one has survived.

Upton Vicarage.
Apr.25. 1855.

Dear Sir,
   I am proposing to try a reformatory experiment in the shape of a cricket club for the young men of this village whose whole time is employed in agriculture and whose mental condition assimilates too nearly to the nature of the soil they are so familiar with. I can only do this thing with the aid of those who derive a much more substantial advantage from the producing elements of this parish than I do myself. Mr. Burnell has given me £1 and other proprietors have contributed handsomely. Can you, on Mr. Sutton's behalf, add another £1 to our funds.
   I remain
   Yours most truly
   Fred. Wm. Naylor.

He had used his first contributions very sensibly, for enclosed with this letter was an A5 size prospectus:

UPTON CRICKET CLUB.

The Members of this Club will meet at Upton once a week during the months of May, June, July, and August.

Persons above the age of fourteen from Upton and the neighbourhood may become members upon payment of one shilling for each year.

Bats, Stumps, and Balls, of the best description, will be provided without cost to the members; and half a pint of ale will be offered to each player before he leaves the ground. The ale will be supplied by the different public houses in the village.

The conditions required of the members are these—that they will not use oaths or bad language in the field; and that they will not resort to a public house upon going away.

It is hoped that every member of the Upton Cricket Club will do his best to ensure its respectability and efficiency.

G. WHITAKER,
F. TRUEMAN,
M. FOSTER,
J. DOUBLEDAY.
} STEWARDS.

J. BERRY,........TREASURER.

These two small pieces of paper tell us a great deal about the vicar and his flock. The root of the problem is probably to be found in the last line of the third paragraph of the prospectus - *'and they will not resort to a public house upon going away'*. There were three public house in Upton - the "Cross Keys" and "French Horn" which survive, and the "Reindeer", a beerhouse. This is now "Hallcroft", a private residence. It stands on the north side of the village green. We can be fairly sure that he had become increasingly concerned about teenage drinking, for the young workers, living in the family home, must have had some money to spare, and little to spend it on. We know from oral tradition that appalling drunkenness was seen in the village before the change in licensing hours in 1914; men would drink till they were penniless, strip off their shirts, sell them on the spot, and drink on. Totally insensible, they would eventually be seen lying on the ground outside. In the case of the "Cross Keys", they might well have rolled into the open sewer on the north side of the main road. Some would drink elsewhere, disappearing from the village for weeks.

Factual evidence of this kind of behaviour can be found in the diaries of Francis Kilvert, a clergyman in Wales and Wiltshire at this time. Some of his diaries were burnt and others mislaid after his death in 1879; when they were published in 1938 they were immediately accorded classic status for their richness of description of Victorian life. In his Welsh parish, Clyro, near Hay on Wye, he writes;

'*...Tuesday, 12th April, 1870. Last night the Swan was very quiet, marvellously quiet and peaceful. No noise, rowing or fighting whatever and no man as there sometimes are lying by the roadside all night drunk, cursing, muttering, maundering, and vomiting.....*'

This is enough in itself to give us the general idea, and to assume that all village inns had their peaceful evenings. But his account of events of the following 19th of October when troublemakers from another village arrived at the Feast Ball leaves no room for doubt whatsoever.

'*...the house was in uproar, the company were fighting all night instead of dancing, and in the morning all the respectable people had black eyes. At that time the inn was very badly conducted, people sat up drinking all night and fought it out in the morning in the road before the inn. Frequently they were to be seen at eleven o'clock in the morning stripped and fighting up and down the road, often having drunk and vomited and wallowed in the inn all night....*'

The Reverend Naylor must have decided that a good long game of cricket, occupying perhaps half of a Saturday, would be a useful and agreeable distraction to fill his young parishioner's spare time. He does not speak very highly of these young men; one feels that there had been discussions in the streets, exhortations from the pulpits, visits to homes, that have not brought the improvements that he wanted. Finally his temper is giving way; having struggled on for fifteen years, this really is his last effort, and then he has done as much as a man can do. If some of the better-off people of the village or nearby would at least dig into their pockets for once, he might just get this new idea off the ground.

He made a good choice of stewards. George Whitaker, aged 50, yeoman farmer, must have been wealthy and shrewd. He owned what was by far the largest farm in the village, 280 acres, and employed five men and a boy. He had six sons, aged 7,9,13,14,18,23, and four daughters. In December that year his wife would conceive a seventh son. His name is first on the list of stewards. He must have been a prime mover and contributor, with a strong ulterior interest in the club beside his philanthropic one, for his sons loved the game, as we shall see, and at least one was to become a strong club cricketer. The family probably lived in the Grange, a fine squarely built Georgian farmhouse on the south of the main road as it leaves Upton for Southwell. He had employed four servants, but as his family grew up he made do with two.

John Doubleday was another of the stewards. He kept the "Reindeer" beer house, farmed 95 acres and employed two workers. He had six children, of whom three still lived with him in 1855, two daughters and a son aged fourteen. Aged 49, he was an active cricketer - a batsman. His son, William Doubleday, farmed 60 acres, most probably at Chapel Farm, which is still a working farm, about two hundred yards west of the "Cross Keys". He was aged 24 at the time, and his sister Sarah worked as his housekeeper. His younger brother George, aged ten, lived with them.

Frederick Trueman was a bricklayer, aged 22. His father and mother, Esmond (45) and Charlotte (44), lived in Upton at Candant House, opposite the "French Horn". They had a building firm. Frederick lived with them at this time. He would become the wicketkeeper - he probably had strong hands. Four of his sons - he also had four daughters - would become mainstays of the club. His eldest son, Walter, would be born thirteen years later, in 1868, and hold various offices until the 1940's. Then would come Ernest, born in 1871, another cricketer. His third son, Henry "Harry" Trueman, would be born in 1874, turn professional, and assist clubs throughout the

country, especially in the Lancashire league, Lincolnshire, and Wales. A fourth son, young Frederick, would be born in 1877. Harry would buy High Farm and farm it until his death. His son Ronald and grandchildren would be an enormous support to the club until the present day.

Matthew Foster was a tailor. He lived in the village centre, between the "Reindeer" and the post office, which occupied the white gabled Corner Farm Cottage. Four houses stood on the village green at the time, and one of these must have been his. He was aged 27; his wife Charlotte was four years older. He had a one-year-old son, Charles, but his wife may have been pregnant with a second, William, and a third, Frederick, was born in 1860.

Of John Berry we know nothing except that he was one of the gentry, and therefore could be trusted with the responsible post of treasurer.

The Reverend Frederick Naylor was now 45. His wife, Maria Anne, was 38. They employed three servants. He could be satisfied that his club had made a good start. The boys that he lodged and taught in the vicarage would also be able to play, and in the fullness of time so would his own son, Frederick, aged seven, and Ellen aged six, could watch... His work for the village could now continue in its dynamic way, as this item of local news from the "Advertiser" of February 23rd, 1859, makes clear.

'MUSICAL ENTERTAINMENT - *An evening concert of a highly interesting character was given by the village choir in the school-room adjoining the vicarage on Monday evening, the 14th inst. The performance consisted of a choice selection of songs, glees, etc., the production of some of the most eminent of modern composers. Some overtures and other instrumental pieces were executed in a brilliant style by Mr. Mason, on the pianoforte, accompanied by Messrs. Cockayne and Flinders on the violin and violincello. A solo by Mr. Flinders elicited the highest admiration, and was warmly encored. The vocalists were Messrs. Foster, Neale, Cobham, and Trueman, who performed their parts in a manner which would not do discredit to professional singers. The attendance was good, and the burst of applause which followed the performance of each piece of music sufficiently indicated the satisfaction and pleasure which was experienced. When the performance was over, the singers and their friends sat down to an excellent supper which had been provided for them, and the expense of which was defrayed by gentlemen residing in the neighbourhood. At the close of the proceedings the Rev. F.W. Naylor congratulated the parties upon whom the management had devolved on the success that had attended their efforts, and observed that it must be a source of intense gratification to themselves to know that they had been the means of promoting innocent enjoyment amongst those around them. He contrasted the state of things in this village now with what they were twenty years ago, and said it was highly gratifying to behold the improvement. He concluded his remarks by throwing out some excellent hints for the use of those who are animated with the idea of self-advancement, and by whom they could not fail to be fully appreciated.'*

Frederick Trueman must have had a fine voice; we know that his son Harry sang tenor. Their names recur in many reports of concerts in Upton. But note that "innocent"; Frederick Naylor did not mince his words; he must have seen far too many examples of the worst kinds of behaviour, and not liked them; he would have had to learn to be cynical, as Kilvert would in Clyro in 1872;

'...Two old women Sarah Jones and Hannah Probert were both lying in bed and groaning horribly. I gave them some money and their cries and groans suddenly ceased.'

On June 29th 1859, the Advertiser at last recognised the team he had founded by printing a match report and scorecard after his Upton cricket side beat Averham by an innings and nine runs. Sadly, he had died a month before, aged 49, and been buried in his own churchyard on May 28th about 25 yards from his front door.

The England team in action in Canada in 1859.

Chapter Two
The First Match

We can be very nearly certain that the field chosen for cricket in Upton was the one that was still in use after the second world war. Church Meadow, or the Bull Meadow, to give it its seventeenth century name, is reached by walking along Church Lane between the church and the vicarage. After the graveyard there is a short downhill walk of perhaps one hundred and fifty yards, and then access was gained by crossing the dyke on a portable wooden footbridge. Until the middle of the twentieth century this bridge was kept in the garden of the house immediately to the north of the church, Meadow View, owned by Mr. Savage, a churchwarden, wheelwright, and coffin maker. It seems likely he made the portable bridge. If a permanent bridge had been placed there it would have created a right-of-way, which the owners of the land opposed. His workshop can still be seen, a single story addition to the south wing of Meadow View, now a lounge. Nearby is a particularly fine example of one of Upton's many wells, five feet in diameter, surrounded by a brick wall. It is at least twenty feet deep and is being excavated by the present owners.

Church Meadow is solid clay, and the field is large enough for three pitches. A shed stood to the right hand side of the footbridge as one faces south across the Trent's flood plain towards the racecourse. That view is rather featureless, but if one looks back towards the church, at the top of its eminence, then the ground's backdrop of church and hillside and trees is a pleasing one.

Was this field used for any other kind of sport? In the sixteenth century Henry the eighth decreed that every man and youth had to practise with the longbow in a field near his village church every week. This regularity of practice guaranteed Henry a good supply of archers for the wars against the French. Bull Meadow would have been the obvious choice for archery, being flat, wide, and offering no danger at all to the inhabitants of the village.

The first games of cricket played on the Bull Meadow would have been immediately recognisable as such to a casual spectator, but a modern cricketer would spot changes. Since the eighteenth century the bowlers - underarm bowlers - had begun to experiment with round arm deliveries; that is to say, the arm came round level with the shoulder, but NOT above it. In 1816 a law was introduced to prohibit this round-arm bowling. John Willes, of Kent, became the first bowler in the game's history to be no-balled for throwing when he opened the bowling for Kent at Lord's on the 15th of July, 1822, using the round-arm method. But by 1827 many bowlers had tried it and the Sussex pair, William Lillywhite and James Broadbridge, had perfected it. Three experimental matches were played between Sussex and England, and the MCC authorised "round-arm" bowling the following year - 1823. But other bowlers were experimenting with OVER-ARM bowling, and that might also be allowed by some umpires. However, Edgar Willsher of Kent was the first to be no-balled for bowling overarm, by John Lillywhite at the Oval on 26th August, 1862, but this was seven years AFTER cricket had begun at Upton. Overarm bowling was finally legalised on 10th June, 1864, but it did not lead to an overnight change in bowling actions. The 1878 Australian team was the first to employ a specialist overarm attack and another decade was to pass before the new style became prevalent. The embryo Upton cricketers were therefore born into the middle of one of only two bowling controversies in the history of the game; the other one, of course, would be the bodyline controversy in Australia in the winter of 1932/1933, in which the most famous Nottinghamshire cricketer of all - Harold Larwood - would be one of the two English protagonists. Mr. Naylor seemed to have had little respect for the youths, judging by the tone of his letter, and probably distanced himself from them; presumably he left the coaching to his stewards, and presumably they coped with this and other problems. Persuading a youth who has spent a long, hot day hoeing turnips, or chasing a cow, that his particular bowling action would not do, whereas his friend's very similar action would, must have been a task for the most dedicated. The steward's charges could have seen the three different bowling actions - under-arm, roundarm, overarm - by walking to the Kelham Road ground in Newark or the Top ground at Southwell, where matches had been played since the 1790's. The fact that one bowling action was illegal, and another only just legal, might have added to the fun, but the cricketers of Upton were not to be rid of the problem for fifty years or more. This we know for certain, because of rule 5 on the back of the fixture card for 1903, regarding practice nights:

>'5. *That 10 minutes batting be taken in rotation, and 10 minutes balling. The balling to be left to the option of the player.*'

This can only refer to the style of bowling.

However, it all came right on Thursday the 23rd of June, 1859, as can be seen by this report in the "Advertiser", the first report we have of any match involving Upton Cricket Club. It had been a very hot summer, and became " excessively so" in July.

UPTON v. AVERHAM. - *A friendly game was played on the 23rd ultimo, between the villages of Upton and Averham, which proved in favour of the former, which will be seen by the score:-*

AVERHAM.

S.Bell, b G.Whitaker	23	st Trueman	37
G.Foster, b G.Whitaker	0	b G.Whitaker	2
R.Lee, b G.Whitaker	1	c F.Trueman,b Neale	1
R.Marsh, b G.Whitaker	0	b G.Whitaker	1
S.Foster, b G.Whitaker	0	c G.Whitaker,b Neale	0
J.Cobham, b.G.Whitaker	0	not out	6
R.Snaith, c J.Whitaker,b E.Neale	6	b G.Whitaker	0
W.Marsh, b G.Whitaker	0	b Neale	3
H.Weightman, b G.Whitaker.	0	st Trueman	0
J.Lee, not out	0	run out	0
H.Harris, c R.Foster, b Neale	2	b G.Whitaker	7
Byes 2, wides 5	7		
Total	37		57

UPTON.

G. Whitaker Esq., b T. Foster	1
J. Whitaker, b T. Foster	9
W. Whitaker, b R. Marsh	42
T. Whitaker, b G. Foster	1
J. Doubleday, st R. Marsh	2
F. Truman, b R. Marsh	0
E. Neale, b Marsh,c S. Bell	6
G. Ulyett, b S. Foster	14
W. Curzon, leg before wicket, b G Foster	0
C. Marshall, b R. Marsh	1
R. Foster, not out	1
Byes 13, wides 13	26
Total	103

This match was probably played on the pitch north of Averham church on the west bank of the Trent. The last pavilion can still be seen - it is now used as a fishing hut. Upton won by an innings and 9 runs. In George Whitaker, Esquire, aged 26, eldest son of the Whitaker family, they had a formidable bowler, even allowing for the fact that the pitch must have been very poor, as pitches always were in the nineteenth century. Eight wickets fell to him in the first innings, and four in the second; it might have been six in the second innings, for Trueman stumped two victims, and wicket-keepers' victims were not credited to the bowler in 1859. Fred Trueman was probably wearing wicket-keeping gloves on his strong bricklayer's hands. These were introduced in about 1850. He could well have been wearing a protective box, introduced by Thomas Box, the Sussex wicket-keeper in the 1830's. The Whitakers probably wore pads and tubular gloves, which had been in use for about twenty years, but lesser fry may have made do with one pad or none.

John Whitaker, aged 22, had a quietish match. Walter Whitaker, aged 18, played the innings of the day, and possibly of the season; 42 runs would not have been scored easily, and Averham seem to have had a strong bowling attack. Averham's S. Bell must have gone home a disappointed man, for he was obviously a consistent batsman of high class, and without his runs Averham would have been annihilated.

The Upton team was a youthful one with the exception of John Doubleday, the club steward and publican at the "Reindeer" aged 53; Thomas Whitaker was 16, Fred Trueman was 26, and William Curzon 21.

What else can be deduced from the scorecard? The cricket historian must emphasise strongly the ability of two of the four Whitakers playing, George and Walter. Clearly they are in a class above all the other players except Bell of Averham. It is most tempting to hypothesise that these three, at least, had learnt the game at grammar schools. We know that the Magnus had a strong side; they played very frequently against the Newark Club and other grammar schools on the Kelham road ground. One speculates that the Whitakers had learnt their game either at public school or the Minster school. They must inevitably have gone to one or the other, given their father's wealth and status: probably the Minster. We know for certain that George had some contact with the leading players of the day with the Southwell club, with its professionals, including John Jackson, the fastest and most feared bowler in England, as this press-cutting of Monday 15th March, 1899, reveals. The newspaper is not known, but might be the Leicester Mercury.

'DEATH OF AN OLD NOTTS SPORTSMAN. It will be of interest to the sporting fraternity to know that after a painful illness there passed away on Wednesday the 8th of March, at Leicester, Mr. George Whitaker, who was well known in the neighbourhood of Southwell and Newark. As an all-round sportsman he was most popular, his favourite pursuits being, shooting, hunting, and cricket. He was the eldest son of Mr. John Whitaker, and was born at Upton, where he frequently made big bags of game with the old muzzle-loader, and in company with the late Mr. Thomas Dufty, being greatly aided by a favourite pointer which Mr. Dufty presented to him. For many years he was a member of the Southwell Cricket Club, who at that time had a very strong team, numbering among their members the great bowlers, Messrs. Jackson and Tinley, and other first class cricketers. He rendered good aid in the frequent encounters with the Notts County team, who at that time had a strong supporter in old Richard Daft. In 1866 he removed to Nottingham, and became the managing partner

in the Carrington Brewery Company (Smith, Bell and Whitaker), after Bell and Whitaker, where he built up a very successful business, but unfortunately was obliged to retire through ill-health after seven years unflagging work. He then came back to Southwell, where, after a few years rest, he again took up the thread of sport. A few years ago he took up his abode in Leicester, where he soon became a well-known character in the cricket field, and was regarded as quite an authority by the young blood on any intricate point of cricket. He followed up his sporting instinct on his farm near the town. On one occasion, whilst showing a friend around the farm, he killed a fox with his walking stick which broke cover from a thick hedge, the fox making many attempts to get away. He was 66 at his decease, and was interred at Knighton, Leicester, being followed to his last resting place by his widow, six sons, and three daughters. His third son, John William Whitaker, died in America a few weeks back. His eldest daughter, Mary Ellen, is living now in America.'

George Whitaker was obviously a strong and resolute character who made the most of the advantages of his birth. It is a pity we do not know more about Walter, who at the age of 18 played the innings of that midsummer Thursday while the rest of the side foundered. We might know a little about Mr. Dufty, however, from this cutting of November 6th, 1872.

'FIRE AT KNAPTHORPE - About three o'clock on Saturday morning a fire broke out in the stackyard on Mr. Dainty's farm (late Mr. Dufty's) which resulted in the almost total destruction of a very large stack of this year's oats and some cloths, the damage amounting to about £200. The fire engine from Southwell was sent for and did good service. The wind was high, but fortunately in a direction to prevent the spread of the fire to other stacks in the yard, or the conflagration must have been of very serious extent. About midnight all was seen safe, and there are certain circumstances which lead to the suspicion that it was the work of an incendiary. On the other hand, the finding of a candle near the stack would almost warrant the more favourable belief that it was caused accidentally by tramps sleeping in the yard.'

This seems to be Knapthorpe Manor Farm, on the road between Southwell and Caunton, perhaps a mile south of Caunton. The farm is in very good hunting and shooting country to this day, as the author can testify, which strengthens the case for this Mr. Dufty being the one mentioned. Mr. Dufty often played cricket for Caunton.

John Jackson's origins are slightly uncertain, though his end is well-documented. It is said that his mother was a gypsy and his father was a titled gentleman. His photograph would support this thesis strongly, for it reveals a strongly featured man of swarthy complexion with black curly hair. We know that originally he lived in Wellow and would walk to Retford or Southwell to play cricket. In 1859 he was at the height of his fame. He had been discovered by "Old" William Clarke while playing for Newark against Clarke's England XI. Clarke spotted his talent and Jackson soon found himself in the Nottinghamshire and England teams. His peak seasons were from 1857 to 1863, when he took 671 wickets in important matches at around ten runs apiece. He travelled the country with "Old" William Clarke's England XI playing against the Twenty-twos of any town which could guarantee a good, admission-paying crowd. Against these local heroes he achieved astonishing bags of wickets; 331 in 1857, 359 in 1858, 346 in 1859. His fame lasted little more than ten years, celebrated in verse and Punch cartoons; but that is a long career in the top-class game for a bowler of express pace, which makes cruel demands of the bowler's muscles and joints. For comparison, Harold Larwood played only 21 tests for England between 1926 and 1932, and Frank Tyson only 17 between 1954 and 1958. Jackson did not salt away the earning of his halcyon years and in the 1890's he was discovered destitute in a Liverpool workhouse - a frail-looking individual with a long white beard, who had once been the terror of the world's batsmen. As an illustration of this point one may quote his figures on the first England tour to America and Canada, which left Liverpool on the 22nd of September,1859. In the four matches played Jackson took 46 wickets for 144 runs - an average of 3.13 in international cricket. Now, Jackson bowled fast over-arm; may George Whitaker have learnt from his friend and also bowled fast over-arm, as opposed to roundarm? One supposes that he did; furthermore, on that Wednesday the cricket-players of Averham received a battering from this gentleman from Upton which, with hindsight, they would recall with pride and ruefulness in later years around the kitchen fire.

Fred Lillywhite, who organised and managed the tour, and scored.

Chapter Three
Sympathy, Science and Strictures; The Work of Churchmen and Landowners

The Reverend Peacock followed the example of dynamic activity set by the Revered Naylor. The Advertiser's columns regularly reported examples of rectitude and improvement for parishioners young and old, as on Wednesday, August 8th, 1860.

'CHURCH SUNDAY SCHOOL ANNIVERSARY. - On Thursday last, the anniversary of the Church Sunday School took place here. The children, to the number of about 50, met at the school-room, and with a bunch of flowers each walked to the Hall, where they sung (sic) several songs and hymns very creditably. They afterwards received their prizes for good conduct and early attendance during the past year. Thence they went into the school and partook of an excellent tea. About 60 friends afterwards took tea together. The children then went to a field and played until nine o'clock, when there was a display of fireworks. Through the kindness of P.R. Falkner, Esq., the children of the Southwell Union Workhouse were invited, and enjoyed themselves very much.'

Similarly, in September 1894, the Sunday School children processed again, but this time from the National School to the church, accompanied by the Reverend W.J. Peacocke and their teachers, and bearing "banners and beautiful bouquets". Books and toys were given as prizes in the vicarage garden after a service and sermon, then games took place in a field lent by Mr. S. Foster. The Sunday school took place in the old tythe barn, now the Parish room, and this seems evidence that it had flourished throughout the nineteenth century.

In October 1862, had come the first reference to the parish's generosity.

'The annual harvest festival was held in the Parish Church on Thursday evening, the 10th inst. Notwithstanding the inclemency of the weather, the service was very fairly attended. A very appropriate sermon was preached by the Rev. J.M. Dolphin, Vicar of Coddington, from the 11th verse of the 12th chapter of Proverbs. The church was decorated in a very seemly manner, reflecting great credit on those persons who had interested themselves in the matter. A new anthem, "Rejoice in the Lord", composed by Sir Geo. Elvey, was sung by the choir in a very creditable manner. At the close of the service a collection, amounting to £4 18s was made, which we understand is to be devoted to the funds of the Newark Hospital and Dispensary.

(October 16th, 1872)

There are repeated references to the decoration of the church and to collections which show that the village was generous to the less fortunate. Thus, November and December, 1874.

'A meeting in aid of the British and Foreign Bible Society was held in the village last Friday evening, the Rev. Mr. Peacock, with his usual ability, acting as chairman. The Rev. Mr. Midwinter, vicar of Bleasby, the Rev. Mr. Mills, vicar of Hockerton, Mr. Willis, of Upton, and the Rev. Mr. Birch, association secretary, addressed the meeting, each eliciting considerable applause. The receipts from all sources for the last year amounted to £8 16s. 10d.'

'Foreign Missions at Upton. On Sunday morning the 22nd ult., an impressive sermon was preached by the Rev. Mr. Peacock, vicar, in this church, and on the following evening the appointed interesting service was observed which was fairly attended. Last Friday evening the annual meeting was held in connection with the above named society, the Rev. Mr. Peacock presiding. The Rev. Mr. Midwinter, vicar of Bleasby, and the Rev. Mr. Hutton, vicar of Norwell, addressed the meeting, and their speeches were received with hearty applause. There was a good attendance, and the total collections with the subscriptions for the past year amounted to £11.12s.2d.'

'The Christmas decorations at Upton Parish Church this year (we noticed) were exceedingly chaste and beautiful. The noble pillars were gracefully wreathed with holly, ivy, and other evergreens. A chancel arch was erected with great taste and skill, surmounted by the text - "Glory to God in the Highest." The pulpit and lectern were elegantly decorated. All must have admired the beautiful design of the font, the text of green berries, done on white wool - "Not by water alone, but by water and blood." The villagers, as well as others, worked with the most hearty good will in making still more beautiful their beautiful parish church windows.'

The church was decorated again in 1875 and again in 1879. Curiously, the 1875 report was identical, but the 1879 one was muted:-

'CHRISTMASTIDE. - This festive season has not passed away without considerable interest being manifested in it, services having been held in the church, which was prettily decorated for the occasion, while the pulpit and font deserve especial mention and reflect the highest credit upon those whose willing hands laboured so assiduously to accomplish the object attained.'

Larger churches in Newark, Grantham, and Retford were also decorated. On September 24th. 1884, it was reported that the church was "embellished with flowers, fruit, and corn" for the harvest festival.

In October, 1887 the Advertiser mentioned that it was decorated by the "Misses Peacocke and other ladies of the congregation with corn, fruit, evergreens, and flowers and well filled by a large congregation.

Mr. Falkener's home, Upton Hall, to which the Sunday school processed, is the one that we see today, rebuilt in stately classical design in 1832, with massive columns supporting a south facing portico. Inside can still be seen one wall from the original building from which Mr. Oglethorpe fled to escape the plague of 1609. Philip R. Falkner was an attorney, aged 58, farming 42 acres of land, born in Southwell in 1802. His interest in the residents of the workhouse is clearly shown, and his humanity and kindness in other matters will be seen later. His wife Alicia, born in Islington, London, was 7 years younger. His son Evelyn was aged 17, an articled clerk to an attorney. Their daughters Mary, 15, Harriet, 9, and Susannah, 7, were described as scholars. Mr. Falkner employed a butler, George Jones, aged 25, and a cook, Emma Shuttleworth, aged 30, who had a kitchen maid, Elizabeth Askew, aged 15. There were three housemaids aged 29, 28, and 15 - Elizabeth Ward, Elizabeth Taylor, and Eliza Cook. The daughters do not seem to have sought work after their education for eleven years later they were described as "landowner's daughters." A governess had joined the household, presumably to educate Susannah. Her name was Katharine Black, and she was Scottish. Evelyn, however, had become a solicitor. Two housemaids had gone and been replaced by one "ladies' maid".

Further evidence of Mr. Falkner's empathy is clearly shown in the Advertiser's first paper of 1868, on January 1st.

'... P.R.Falkner Esq., of Upton Hall, according to his annual custom, has given to a dozen poor people half a ton of coals each, which will prove a very acceptable gift at this festive season of the year.'

A year later one sees that the size of the gifts was subject to sympathetic upward review.

'Last week, according to his annual custom, P.R. Falkener, Esq., of Upton Hall, gave to fourteen poor aged people, most of them widows and residents of Upton, half a ton of coal each, delivered free by his own teams.'

So the wagons that carried grain in summer went to Ollerton in December and came back full of coal.

A suggestion of the eminence of the village in local farming is seen in this report from the Advertiser just two months later, in the autumn.

' ... FARMING SOCIETY - This very useful and prosperous society held its fifth anniversary at Winkbourne (sic), on Tuesday,

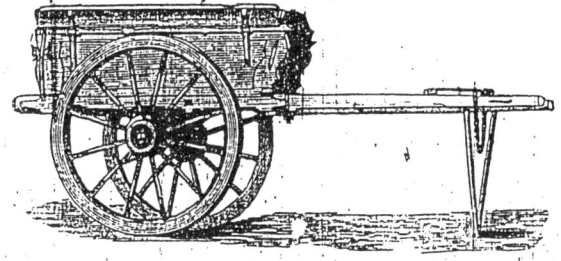

TRENT BRIDGE WORKS (NEAR MIDLAND STATION) NEWARK.

STEPHENSON'S

CORN AND TURNIP DRILLS.	CHAFF CUTTERS.
PLOUGHS.	HORSE GEARS.
LAND ROLLERS.	REAPING and MOWING MACHINES.
DRAGS.	HORSE RAKES.
HARROWS.	WEIGHING MACHINES.

PRIZE CARTS WITH MACHINE MADE WHEELS,
ALL WARRANTED TO BE MADE OF GOOD DRY MATERIAL

the 16th of October. The president, E.V.P. Burnell, was unavoidably absent, the chair was most ably filled by Major Boddam, of Kirklington Hall, supported by W.H. Barrow, Esq., M.P., J. Marriot, Esq., Bleasby. and most of the neighbouring gentry and farmers. The Chairman gave all the usual toasts; and he, as well as Mr. Barrow, most ably set forth the great usefulness and benefit generally to all classes of these societies. The ploughing took place in a field in the occupation of Mr. Savage the vice-president, on the Orchard Wood Farm. The judges of the ploughing were Mr. Truswell, Mr. H. Marriott and Mr. Curtis, who stated the work generally was performed in a most satisfactory manner; and the great improvement in this branch of agricultural labour is mainly owing to these meetings. There were 46 entries in the various classes. The chairman presented a beautiful silver cup, the gift of the president, to Cornelius Adam Clarke, son of Mr. Clarke, of Hockerton, the successful competitor in the ploughing class for farmer's sons. S. Richmond, of Fiskerton, and Jos. Elstone, of Hockerton, were highly commended in the same class. The judges for draining and scotching were Mr. Henderson and Mr. M.J. Milward. The Hon. Secretary, Mr. Bradwell, gave to each successful competitor an illustrated card to enable them to receive the amount of their prizes. They were afterwards addressed by the Chairman. An excellent dinner was produced by Mr. and Mrs. Ricket. The whole of the labourers had a very substantial one after the work was completed. The show of mangol wurzel was not so fine as last year. Mr. Hardy, Mr. Adams, and Mr. Bradwell exhibited very good Swede turnips and carrots.'

The president, E.V.P.Burnell, is the man who was asked for £1 by the Reverend Naylor to found the club. This also explains the Reverend's caustic reference in his letter to those who "derive a much more substantial advantage from the producing elements of this parish than I do myself" - did he ask the other leading members of the society for financial help? He must have thought that they should do more for the welfare of their young labourers than provide one large free meal a year. But in Mr. Burnell's case the jibe is unfair. He was sensitive to the needs of the poor. Thus December 31st, 1873:

'WINKBURN - During Christmas the poor of this village have partaken liberally of the bounties which are usually distributed at this season of the year by E.V.P. Burnell, Esq. A fine beast was fed and killed for the purpose, and each family was supplied with a large piece of beef, and also with half a ton of coals.

In Upton the search for improvement had not slackened.

'LECTURE BY DR. BEEVOR. - On Friday evening week the Vicarage Schoolroom was crowded by an attentive audience, during the delivery of a lecture by Dr. Beevor, of Newark, on "Food, Air, and Water." The Doctor's popular though somewhat novel way of dealing with the subject caused it to prove very attractive, and at the same time exceedingly instructive. Many popular errors were exposed, and explanations were given of many points which are but very imperfectly understood even by those who consider themselves remarkably intelligent. The Doctor was cordially thanked for his services, and it is hoped he will shortly give another lecture in the same place.'

It is possible to note condescension in the tone of this report. Was it written by the Reverend Peacocke, and printed verbatim? One feels that it was, for provincial newspapers could not and cannot afford to place reporters in every parish hall, or substantially alter a text; surely these are the Reverend's words. Rhetorical points seem to be being made in the phrase "Many popular errors" and also in the clause "who consider themselves remarkably intelligent." The Reverend was obviously prepared to struggle for progress as his predecessor did; and if his lowly flock thought they were educated already, they must be disabused, because scientific knowledge takes a long time to acquire; he obviously has other important lectures on the way which will have to be fully digested. And so it proved. Scarcely six weeks later more useful advice was offered, and a significant improvement revealed.

'RURAL LIBRARY. On Tuesday this week the usual annual tea in connexion (sic) with the Upton Rural Library was held in the

Schoolroom. After the members and subscribers and other friends from Southwell and the villages round about had finished the large and bountiful supply of cake and tea placed before them, and the tables having been cleared away to make room for others who wished to come and listen to the music and speeches, the Rev. Wm. Jas. Peacocke (the vicar) after making a short but impressive speech, read the account of how the library had gone on during the past year. He then called on the Rev. J. F. Mills (Hockerton), who made an ingenious speech on "Spectacles", pointing out which people wear when young and think everything innocent, when old and distrustful, or when both wear when jealous. The Rev. John Conington (Southwell), and Mr. Geo. Foster (Upton), also addressed a few words to the meeting. During the evening several songs were sung by members of the choir with the help of some ladies and Mr. Irons (Southwell) with great success: one called "Bye and bye" giving especial pleasure and affording great amusement to those who heard it.'

This report is disappointing in that it omits details of what the library had done. One sees again the inevitable separation of the classes - some people seemed to have waited outside until all the good things had been finished by the "Members and subscribers." The reporting of the speech about spectacles suffers because of poor grammar, probably on the part of the sub-editor. That the tea was an established event, and the library a success, seems to be certain, for we have a very similar report in 1865, four years later.

'A public tea party in connection with the Upton Rural Library was held in the village school room on Friday week. The room was very tastefully decorated and a goodly number sat down to tea. After tea several addresses were delivered by clergymen and others; there were agreeably diversified by the efforts of the church choir, who assisted by two of the boys from the Southwell Minster, sang a selection of glees, carols, &c. The worthy Vicar, the Rev. J. Peacocke, presided, and on the platform we noticed the Revs. J. Conington, Southwell; W.J.Marsh, Bleasby; -- Mills, Hockerton; and J.G. Wright, Nottingham. The latter gentleman gave an interesting address on the homely phrase, "I keep myself to myself". The Rev. J.W. Marsh followed with an able and suitable one on "Labour and Leisure". The Rev. Mills chose as the subject of his address "Nothing;" and was followed by the Rev. J. Conington, who in lieu of an address, exhibited the magnesium light, which seemed to astonish and please the Upton folk very much. Altogther a very agreeable evening was spent, and we have no doubt the next meeting of a similar character will be looked

forward with pleasure by the inhabitants of Upton. The chairman announced that, acting upon the principle of "Better Late than never," it was intended to commence a series of Penny Readings, similar to those at Southwell and other towns, the first to take place on Wednesday, the 15th instant.'

The interest in penny readings had been sweeping the country since Charles Dickens began his enormously successful public readings of selections from his own works in theatres in 1858. Similarly, selections from literature were read in local halls by local dignitaries to any audience who had paid a penny for admission. Dickens, ever the frustrated actor, put so much emotion and feeling into his readings, especially the death of Little Nell, that he was emotionally and physically drained by the end of his performance; so much so, that he was advised for the good of his health, not to continue them, or at least not to read the death scene. He ignored this advice, and it is certain that the strain of his last tour hastened his death in 1870.

We can gain a very good idea of what the Upton penny readings might have been like from Kilvert's diary on February 3rd, 1871.

'This evening we had our fourth penny reading. The room was fuller than ever, crammed, people almost standing on each other's heads, some sitting up on the high window seats. Many persons came from Hay, Bryngwyn and Painscastle. Numbers could not get into the room and hung and clustered round the windows outside trying to get in at the windows. The heat was fearful and the foul air gave me a crushing headache and almost stupefied me. I recited Jean Ingelow's "Reflections" and my own "Fairy Ride."'

Again, on 23rd January of the following year, Kilvert writes;
'The Penny Reading tonight went off admirably, one of the very best we have ever had. A crowded room, nearly 250 people.'

Although the Advertiser's article makes no mention of the fact, the Upton Penny Readings were probably the first public event held in the new school. An important clue is that it is described as the "village" schoolroom for the first time. Once again the clergymen seem to have agreed on a mixture of moral precepts and science as a suitable curriculum for the evening.

In January, 1867, evidence clearly shows that the library was both established and valued.

'UPTON LIBRARY - The annual meeting in connection with this institution was held on Tuesday, the 22nd, in the Sunday School-room, Upton, when about 130 sat down to tea. This library is one of the twenty which were founded by the Rev. F.W.

Naylor, the lamented vicar of the parish. Tea being over the Rev. W. J. Peacocke took the chair, and after reading a statement of the accounts, gave a short epitome of the principal events which had occurred in the parish during the past year. He then called upon Mr. E.S. Faulkner to read a report of the state of the Upton penny Bank; after which several excellent songs were sung by the choir, assisted by friends, Mr. Irons, the organist of Southwell Minster, kindly presiding at the piano. The Rev. J. Conington and the Rev. J. W. Marsh also made appropriate speeches, and the proceedings were brought to a close about ten o'clock.'

The parish room must have been packed, and there cannot have been very much room for the tea. Space would have been at a premium, especially when one remembers that there was a stage at the west end of the room on which the clergy would have sat. The room is well-filled when about seventy members and friends spread themselves out for a modern cricket club supper. Such a large number could only be accommodated if the meeting was seated on benches and the tables were fairly narrow. The legal maximum is one hundred now, but this is for an enlarged premises; a large kitchen extension was completed in 1990 to bring the hall up to the requirements of the European Parliament. What stands out from this report, however, is the astonishing achievement by the Reverend Naylor in founding twenty libraries. Founding and running one library is work enough for a man; he must have possessed very considerable qualities indeed. In March, 1880, the Advertiser reports another Library tea, and prints the programme of 13 songs and readings, commenting *'quite an event in the village...the advantages of having a well-stocked library in their midst seem to be appreciated by the villagers.'* Again, in May 1895, another successful concert took place, this time containing 14 items, the last of which was the "Toy Symphony" by Romberg, by an orchestra under the baton of the vicar's daughter.

The Penny Bank was in Queen Street, Southwell, until long after the second world war, immediately west of Gadsby's the bakers. No interest was paid and the money had to be withdrawn the week before Christmas. A typical investment might have been a shilling. It is interesting that the younger Mr. Faulkner appears to have had charge of it, and one speculates that the Upton branch was based in a room in the Hall.

The promised Penny Reading, or something similar, seems to have occurred about a week later.

'On Wednesday in last week, in the vicarage schoolroom, a

musical and reading entertainment was given in aid of the sufferers by the recent explosion at Barnsley. The Rev. W. Peacocke, the Vicar, was in the chair, who commenced the proceedings by stating that the meeting was twofold, to give the parishioners a little harmless amusement, and at the same time to afford them an opportunity of contributing to the relief fund. He said there were 700 women and children left helpless by the calamity, and that a very large sum was still required for their assistance. Though the rain descended very heavily all the evening, most of the inhabitants attended and seemed highly delighted with what they heard. The readers and singers were Mr. Evelyn Falkner, of Upton Hall and Messrs. Stenton, Minkley, J.H. Bradwell, Townrow, and Bollon, of Southwell. Mr. J.W. Cooke presided at the piano.'

Attendances at these readings may have been astonishing; one turns again to the Reverend Kilvert in Clyro.

'I hear that last night there were some 60 people standing outside the school during the whole time of the Readings. They were clinging and clustering round the windows, like bees, standing on chairs, looking through the windows, and listening, their faces tier upon tier. Some of them tried to get through the windows when the windows were opened for more air.'

The explosion at Barnsley was in a pit, and 350 men had been killed. Again the parishioners were encouraged to give financial help. An error has crept in, however, for the inference is that most of the village attended; this would have been impossible, for the population was 600. One sees again that the younger Mr. Falkener took a leading role, and was assisted by "Mr. Stenton" and others. This seems very likely to have been either the father or grandfather of Sir Frank Stenton, the great historian. His "Anglo-Saxon England" was the definitive work on the period for most of the twentieth century. The family lived at Stenton House, Westgate, which is opposite Lowes Wong.

A benefit concert was given for a cricketer in May,1881. Abraham Cooling had suffered "three long illnesses and been otherwise unfortunate". The Misses Peacocke, Faulkner, and Brodhurst performed, with others. The concert was organised by two cricketing families, the Wollatts and Savages.

The Wesleyan movement was very strong in the Victorian era, particularly in terms of the construction of chapels. A magnificent example with the typical horseshoe shaped upper gallery is still in use in Southwell, a few yards to the west of the "Saracen's Head." This was built in 1839. A splendid northern extension was started in 1995 and finished in 1996. Another splendid example in Barnbygate, Newark, was totally refurbished in 1995. A very small, plain chapel had been built in Upton in 1831 by the entrance to Chapel Farm. It was well supported if one may judge by this article of November 13th, 1867.

'CHAPEL RE-OPENING The Wesleyan chapel of this village having been closed for some time for the purpose of undergoing considerable alterations, was re-opened on Friday last, when sermons were preached on the occasion afternoon and evening, by the Rev. M. Randles, of Lincoln. The congregations were large and highly respectable. The collections realized over £24. The Rev. W.R. Cockill is appointed to occupy the pulpit at the concluding services next Sunday.'

The chapel was last used in February, 1970, when it was re-opened for the christening of Malcolm Yates, the youngest son of the farmer, Oliver Yates. It had also been re-opened five years before for the christening of Alastair, his older brother. It had closed for regular worship in about 1960, but a Methodist Sunday School ran for a few more years under the leadership of Jack Chester, the last steward of the church and an opening bat for the club. After this the Pentecostal movement expressed interest in using the chapel, and attempted to start a Sunday School, but this came to nothing.

One wonders what the alterations had been. One window has been bricked up at some time; perhaps the present pews were fitted, and the tiny porch added, or perhaps it needed a new roof at that time. Little else could have been done to a building that would scarcely seat a hundred. The article is revealing; the Methodist ministers were obviously keen to maintain a strong empathy with their flock. They saw themselves as visiting preachers, perhaps twenty miles from their own church, passing on the Wesleyan message; not guardians, preceptors, educators, or agents of social change. Their congregations responded very generously indeed, - the weekly wage of an agricultural labourer was about forty pence - but the huge sum collected should be seen in the light of re-opening after a long closure, reaffirmation of faith and purpose, and the need to meet. Other denominations were also active, though perhaps without the advantage of their own church building.

'The Primitive Methodists in this village held their annual missionary meeting last Thursday evening. The addresses were very interesting and the collection liberal. The box of one collector contained the handsome sum of £1.8s. last year and £1. 9s. 8d. this.'

Chapter four
The Harsher Side of Life

Occasionally mundane incidents in the life of the parish were reported in the Advertiser, as on Wednesday 28th March, 1867. To modern eyes it has an almost comical element until one remembers that a crippling injury might have been sustained, or surgery needed. In 1867 general anaesthetics had only recently become widely used. Chloroform had been in use since 1847 for childbirth, amidst strong disapproval. Many thought it unnatural that women should not feel pain during childbirth. However, chloroform received the stamp of royal approval when Queen Victoria accepted it when she gave birth to Prince Leopold in 1853. Previously surgery had been limited to essential operations, such as amputations or the removal of gangrenous limbs, which were performed in three to five minutes, the unfortunate patients being strapped down and held by burly assistants. Anaesthesia opened the way for a wide range of operations of a kind and duration that could not have been performed on conscious subjects, such as the removal of diseased organs. However, the surgeon's art was severely restricted because of the often fatal outcome of infection in the operation wound. Antiseptics were first used successfully in surgery by Joseph Lister in Glasgow in 1865. The mortality rate after major surgery had been 45%, but by 1867 it had begun to drop to a figure of 15%. Carbolic acid was the antiseptic used.

'UNPLEASANT PREDICAMENT - On Monday morning week, as Mr. Joseph Marriott, of Upton Mill, was driving along Easthorpe, Southwell, his pony took fright, and ran with great force against the pillar of one of the gas company's lamps, which instantly severed the axle and wheels from the wicker-work vehicle. The affrighted animal dashed forward at a furious rate in the direction of Newark, making it very difficult for Mr. Marriott to maintain an upright position in the basket; he however maintained his dangerous position on the seat with the most perfect sang froid, until he saw a good opportunity of springing over the side of the vehicle, a feat he accomplished, retaining the reins. Alighting on his feet he ran alongside beside his contumacious quadruped, and before arriving at the White Lion had checked his mad career without further damage.'

Easthorpe is particularly narrow by the "Bramley Apple" public house, and it might well have been there that the gas standard was struck. The "White Lion" still stands on the sharp left hand bend where the road to Fiskerton turns right. Mr. Marriott must have known that if his horse's flight had not been stopped before that bend

it might well have careered into the gasworks, which were but a hundred yards further down the road to Upton on the east side.
Eight years later two other travellers were taken by surprise.

'CARRIAGE ACCIDENT: On Friday evening last, at Southwell, as Mr. Smith, of the Saracen's Head Inn, Newark, and Mr. Ellis, corn merchant, of the same place, were leaving Southwell in a dog cart they met with a serious mishap at the bottom of Easthorpe, Southwell, near to the Gas Works. At this spot there is a round curve in the road, and as Mr. Ellis, who was driving was not acquainted with the road he drove into the hedge. The two gentlemen were pitched out of the trap with considerable force, and Mr. Smith sustained serious injuries to the left leg, some of the guiders being broken. Mr. Ellis was not hurt.

The next accident happened to a boy.

'GUN ACCIDENT AT UPTON - On Friday evening about eight o'clock (14th June, 1867) an accident through playing with firearms, occurred at Upton, near Newark. It appeared that Thomas Cooper, a boy of about fourteen years of age, son of George Cooper, gardener at Upton Hall, was playing with several other boys in Mr. Foster's stackyard, when one of his companions, named Albert Edward Foster said he would fetch his gun out to shoot at his birds, (meaning his playmates.) He accordingly fetched the gun, which was not capped, and he believed not loaded. After playing with it for a time he got a cap and put on for the purpose of making a report, and pointing the barrel at one of the lads he pulled the trigger, when to his astonishment, the gun discharged, and the contents of the barrel lodged in Cooper's right arm. As soon as the accident happened Mr. Falkener despatched a messenger to Southwell for Mr. Calvert, surgeon, who was quickly in attendance, but as it appeared very doubtful whether the arm would not have to be amputated, it was thought advisable to remove him to Newark hospital, where he arrived about midnight. Mr. Calvert accompanied him, and a consultation was held by him and Mr. Appleby, the house surgeon, and Messrs. Lacey, Job, Matterson, and Greenwood, the honorary surgeons of the institution, when it was decided that the only course open to them was to amputate the arm above the elbow, which operation was soon afterwards successfully performed, and the poor boy is now progressing as satisfactorily as can be expected. We understand the gun had been loaded about two years.

The family lived at Cooper's Cottage, set back from the road opposite the French Horn. George Cooper, the gardener, was fifty-one at the time. His wife, Sarah, was eight years older. Thomas lived through his ordeal but employment such as gardening and manual work was closed to him. In the 1871 census he is described as a scholar. It is difficult to say exactly in which farm the accident occurred, but Edward Foster, the father of Albert, owned the second largest farm in the village. He had three sons and two daughters of whom Albert was the oldest, and employed three servants. Thomas Cooper was the victim of a silly youth who should have known much better; the actual cause of the accident is absolutely clear. The "cap" referred to was a percussion cap which exploded when struck by the gun's hammer. It had to be placed upside down over a small nozzle on top of the gun barrel, through which a tiny hole led to the chamber, where the gunpowder and pellets had been waiting for two years. This system, a huge improvement on the flintlock, had been invented two years previously by a man whose name is still with us - Alfred Nobel.

The next victims were beyond medical aid. In the report on the circumstances of the death of Hannah Doubleday in March 1878 one senses stubbornness, ignorance, and a lack of imagination.

A WOMAN BURNT TO DEATH - At the Cross Keys Inn, at Upton, on Saturday last, an inquest was held before Mr. William Wallis, the deputy coroner, touching the death of Hannah Doubleday, who met with her death under the following circumstances:- Richard Doubleday, a woodman, residing at Upton Lodge, Upton, said the deceased was his wife, and she was 61 years of age. He went to his work about seven o'clock in the morning, and he did not return from the wood until he was called away at twelve. When he left home in the morning his wife was in the house alone. She did not complain of illness, but had been subject to fits for the last twenty years and upwards. Sometimes she had one or two fits a day, and then no more for a week or so. She had a fit in bed on Thursday night the 14th inst., he had often tried to persuade her to have a woman with her in the house, on account of her fits, but she was not willing to have one. They lived in a detached house. She could generally tell when the fits were coming on, and always got away from the fire. When he was called from his work, and reached the house, his wife was sitting in her chair. She said she was dying. Mrs. Lawson was in the house when he got home. He sent for Mr. Osborne, surgeon. She died at ten minutes past five on the same day. He noticed that her clothing was burnt. He did not know how she got on fire. - Mary Ann Hutton, of Upton, said deceased came into Mrs. Measure's shop on the morning of the 15th inst. She was alone, and appeared cheerful and did not complain of illness. - Mary Lawson, wife of Joseph Lawson, a labourer of Upton, said she knew the deceased, who was subject to fits. A Mrs. Sherry called to her from the lane, and asked her to go to Mrs. Doubleday, as she thought she was on fire. She went to the house and found her sitting in a chair, with all her clothes burnt off except her stockings. She said she was dying. Witness could see she was badly burnt, but did not tell her so. The husband was the first to come to the house after her, and then Mary Parlby. Deceased was wrapped in wadding and a blanket, and got to bed. She died the same day. - Susan Ann Sheriff, wife of Eli Sheriff who lived at Lambley, and was a chimney sweep, said, on Tuesday she came to her mother's house at Upton Lodge; and as she was passing Doubleday's house she noticed something on fire near the fence, a few yards from the house. Saw some smoke coming from the back window of the house. She shouted fire to a young man. He asked her why she did not go into the house? She did not go because she was frightened. The man had two horses and said he could not leave them. She asked the last witness to go and see what was the matter and she went. - James Rick, a labourer, in the employ of Mr. George Doubleday, said he knew the deceased, and she was subject to fits. Yesterday he was working about 200 yards from Doubleday's house. He had a little boy named Fred Flowers with him. The boy called his attention to the smoke in Doubleday's yard. He told the boy to go and see what was the matter. He went, and brought back word that there was something burning in the yard. Sheriff called to him before the boy got back. He saw Mrs. Lawson going to the house. He did not leave the horses to go to the house, because the boy could not take charge of them. - Mary Parlby, wife of George Parlby, woodman, said she went to Doubleday's house, and found deceased sitting in a chair. She assisted to lift her upstairs. She asked her how it had happened, and she said, "She was going to have some tea, and she felt a fit coming on, and she went out of doors and found herself in flames, and layed down." She did not say any more. The tea pot handle had been burnt off. She was sensible to the last. - Mr. Osborne, surgeon, of Southwell, said when he reached the house he found deceased downstairs and dressed and with a blanket over her shoulders. He examined her, and found the burns were extensive over her face, arms, legs, and body. She was suffering great pain. He inquired how it took place, but could not make anything of her statement. She said, she wanted her left hand cutting. He ordered her to bed, and her wounds were dressed. He saw she could not survive long. She died from the effects of the burning, and the shock to her system. She must have been on fire a long time, as everything was burnt off. - The jury returned the following verdict: "Accidentally burnt to death by falling on the fire in a fit."'

Upton Lodge is a rather isolated house on the northern boundary of the village beside the Newark-Mansfield Road. The ploughman, James Rick, appears unsympathetic or callous in the report, but he was probably an uneducated man, and his employer's horses were his life and existence. He worked with them throughout the week, and would spend much of his free time grooming them at the weekend; there might be no other interest. The deaths of girls and women after their long skirts caught fire was an omnipresent fact of life in the days when the open fire was the centre of family life, and there was a mantlepiece up above it which was a useful place to keep things. Richard Doubleday would have been working in Cheveral Wood.

Nearly a year later a jury had to re-assemble, this time at the "French Horn".

SUICIDE AT UPTON - *An inquest was held at the French Horn, Upton, on Monday evening, before Mr. W. Newton, Coroner, on the body of Sarah Jayes, aged 35, who committed suicide under the circumstances narrated in the following evidence:- Joseph Gill said the deceased was the wife of Wilson Mortimer Jayes, butler at Kirklington Hall. She had been staying with them on the ground of ill-health. She had Dr. Osborne to attend her. On Sunday morning at one o'clock he saw her alive. During the night she came downstairs. He was in bed, but had not got his clothes off because she was so restless. She came down for a little milk. He told her to go to bed and see if she could compose herself. She said, "I will go and try," and went upstairs. She was sleeping in a room with the infant child only. About half an hour afterwards he suddenly thought whether she had gone to bed. He went to look, and saw the window open, and saw she was not in bed. He judged she had gone through the window. He shouted to his sister, and went to look, and found no traces of her. He called her up and down the lanes and fields. Ultimately they found her in the well on the opposite side of the wall. They had no suspicions that she would commit suicide. She got out of the window once before. She was very desponding and had lost all interest in her children. - Mr. J.H. Osborne, surgeon, said he knew the deceased and attended her at Kirklington Hall. He found her excited, and complaining of her stomach, and showing*

dyspeptic symptoms. He advised change, and suggested she should go home to her sister and father, and she was anxious to go. He had attended her since. He saw her a short time ago. He thought her better, and found her cheerful, quiet, and intelligent. He was not aware that she was desponding. She had no internal complaint that he was aware of. He advised her not to take opiates or spirits, but to use them if she required anything. He thought, from her state of health, that she had destroyed herself, and was not responsible for her actions. - The jury returned a verdict of "Suicide whilst in a state of temporary insanity."'
Joseph Gill seems to have done all that a father could do.

Scarcely two years later, in August, 1882 another jury was assembled at the "French Horn". Robert Collingham, a gentleman aged about 40 who lived alone in Upton except for a housekeeper, and who had suffered a stroke two years previously, had ridden to Averham with the Weightmann's to look at some stock at their farm. He then rode back towards Upton, leaving the Weightmann's at the Flash, and proceeding towards Averham Park; no-one knew what happened next. As the Advertiser wrote, *'a number of rumours were afloat as to how the deceased met his death, and a good deal of interest was manifested in the enquiry'...* It gave his housekeeper, Sarah Williams, the chance to reveal a home truth. She told the inquest;

'The Messrs. Weightmann came between ten and eleven and had some sherry....they only drank beer for dinner. The deceased was not quite sober when he left home, but I have seem him much worse. He had brandy and water before he left home ... the Messrs. Weightmann were quite sober..'

John H. Weightmann did not deny those facts and added, *'he had a glass or two of beer at Mr. Machin's, but did not dismount....'*
Mr J.H.Osborne, surgeon of Southwell, had the final word.
'He had a small wound on the lower part of the head, ... he was black in the face and breathing stertorously ... I considered it a hopeless case. I have made a post-mortem examination this day - there were two large clots of blood on the brain, which were the cause of death ... he had, in my opinion, died from an attack of apoplexy, and the fall had nothing to do with it.'

Finally, one notes the Advertiser's attitude in these reports, the first from 1867.

'ROLLESTONE - A MAN IN THE STOCKS - A few days ago the long unused stocks of this village were again made use of to punish a man named William Bartham, a native of this place, who had been convicted of drunkenness and had not paid the

fine after having more than reasonable time allowed. He endured his position six hours with tolerable content, and to the great amusement of spectators. The last person who was put in these stocks until this illustrious gentleman, was a woman named Breckney who got drunk and smashed the crockery 46 years ago.'

More than a century on we see the role of a newspaper differently; here one might say that it is on the mob's side, content to jeer the local drunkard, and to remind the Breckney family and their friends of an unfortunate and almost forgotten incident. There is another instance of the Advertiser seeming at one with the mob, even to the extent of gleeful anticipation, on July 22nd, 1874.

'NOVEL DISTURBANCES AT SOUTHWELL - On Thursday evening the old custom of "Riding the Stang" was revived at Southwell, and the novel proceedings created considerable excitement in the streets wherein they occurred. It is stated that a painter and his wife have not lived recently on very amicable terms, coolness and disregard taking the place of kindness and affection. The other evening high words were used on both sides, and the culminated in a bout with the fists, the husband attacking his better half and beating her severely. News of the domestic differences rapidly spread, and the old mode of expressing disapproval of wife assaults was resorted to. On Thursday night a company more numerous than select met together and provided themselves with tin pans and other unmusical articles. The best "musicians" led the way, and, followed by an admiring company, they proceeded in the direction of the offender's dwelling, beating their kettles and pans at a furious rate. The wife-beater was serenaded and treated gratuitously to an artistic musical performance. It was some minutes before the artistes had finished their task, but directly they had done so the company dispersed, apparently highly delighted with the night's entertainment. It was unofficially intimated that the programme would be repeated another evening.

The use of artistes suggests that this involved the fairer sex.
One must take a balanced view. Until 1868 public executions, and the last hours and minutes of the victim were minutely reported by all newspapers, including the Advertiser. After that date executions took place inside gaols, but the press were allowed in to watch and report everything. There were also frequent accounts of deaths inside Southwell's House of Correction on Burgage Green; prisoners either fashioned cords from lengths of cotton, or used a scarf to suspend themselves from waterpipes or clothes hooks. It was not unusual for

the bodies of newly-born infants to be found in ditches by the workhouse near Galley Hill. The Advertiser did not spare the details. In this context one can see "Riding the Stang" in context. The custom may have more serious origins; "stang" is the present participle of the Old English verb "stingan" - to stab; "stang" means stabbing.

Chapter five
Cricket in the Sixties and Seventies

The "Newark Advertiser" began to print the results of cricket matches at all levels in the 1850's. Any match played at Trent Bridge against another county was likely to be reported at up to two columns length. The scorecards of a few local matches were printed; matches at Newark, Southwell, The Magnus School, Caunton, Winkburn, Mapleback, Retford, Sutton, Rollestone, Fiskerton, Balderton, Trent Iron Works, Newark Watermill, Kneesall, Kirklington, and Averham were included regularly. In fact, it would not be untrue to say that almost every village from Collingham and Laxton in the north to Southwell and Farnsfield seemed to have a team, and to submit reports and scorecards. "Fun" matches, such as Married v. Single, or Maltsters v. Millers were also printed. But until 1879 the only matches featuring Upton are away games, and the inescapable fact is that no-one in Upton could be bothered to send a copy of a home scorecard. "Old" Clarke's All-England Team also had their scorecards printed, as were the Nottinghamshire scorecards, and long reports written. Test match cards and reports were also printed from 1877 onwards. This report and second scorecard featuring Upton appeared at the top of a column on the last (eighth) page of the paper on Wednesday, August 6th, 1862.

CAUNTON v UPTON - This match was played at Caunton on Thursday, July 31st, but was not finished, in consequence of the very unfavourable state of the weather. The following was the score at the time the stumps were drawn:-

```
                         CAUNTON
C. Wragg, b Foster................5    not out....................22
H. Mason, b Foster................0    b Cobham...................10
F. Freer, c Doubleday, b Cobham...0    b Foster ...................9
T. Dufty, run out.................0    b Cobham....................0
W. Richards, b Cobham.............0    c Doubleday, b Foster ......4
W. Mason, st Collingham, b Cobham.7    b Uylett....................7
Rev. S.R. Hole, b Foster..........0
J. Hole, b Foster.................5    c Cobham, b Foster..........0
H. Franklin, b Cobham.............0    run out.....................1
S. Morris, not out................3    run out....................25
C. Neale, run out.................1
Byes 5, wides 7..................12    Byes 14, wides 7...........21
         Total................33                Total..............99
                          UPTON
W. Collingham   b Neale..........10
H. Weightmann, b Neale ...........4
J. Lee, b Mason...................0
G. Foster, not out...............29
J. Cobham, b Neale................1
G. Ulyett, b Neale................7
G. Doubleday.b Neale..............2
T. Cullen, b Neale................7
G. Parlby, b Mason................1
J. Johnson, b Neale...............0
J. Gibson, leg b w, b Neale.......0
Byes 4, leg byes 2, wides 2......69
```

Above: The Old Vicarage, rebuilt for the Reverend Frederic William Naylor in 1840. The gable to the left of the front door marks the position of the earlier Jacobean building.

Left: The Reverend William James Peacocke. He succeeded the Reverend Naylor in 1859, and resigned in 1908.

The Averham team in 1898, photographed in front of Averham church.
Back row: l to r; Harry Lee, unknown, Preston Lee, Harry Trueman, Bill Oldham (the Averham Blacksmith). **Front row:** 1 to r; Herbert Sutton, Mr Webb (the Kelham Estate Agent), The Reverend Wilfred Walker (seated on ground), Fred Lee, "young" Frederick Trueman, unknown, Mr Cobham (the Averham schoolmaster).

The "Old Post Office" in about 1900.
The right hand side of the building is long demolished.
It was a bread and flour shop. The left hand end was a billiards room.
The Norfolk reed for the thatch was fetched from Southwell station.

An Upton team in about 1900.
They appear to be playing on the modern ground in Hockerton Lane.
The young Frederick Trueman is the wicket-keeper.

The school children by the front door. The writing on the slate seems to suggest that it is the first year of King Edward the Seventh's reign, 1901.

The school in 1986.
The cottage which was occupied by the teachers stands at the front of the playground.

"Daddy Upton" and a flock of cross-bred sheep.
The "French Horn" to the right of the picture. See appendix G.

"Daddy Upton" and Caudwell's dray at the junction with Hockerton Lane.
See appendix G.

A wedding in 1909, taken from the "French Horn" steps.
Mabel Mildred Trueman married Thomas Batty. Candant House is in the back ground.
Her sisters Kate and Lottie are the bridesmaids. Harry Trueman is to their left
in a bowler hat. Walter Trueman can be seen on the path smoking a pipe.

Upton Mill from the west.

Upton Hall. The stables and coach houses.

Upton Hall. The ballroom.

Mabbott's forge at the top of Carr Dyke Lane.

*The Collies Charity cottage.
Intended for the village's oldest resident. For many years the home
of the midwife, who went about her duties on a tricycle.*

Caunton is a village similar in size to Upton, about five miles to the north on the Ollerton-Newark road. The Upton team contains only G. Ulyett of the side that played Averham in 1859. This shows a considerable lack of continuity, for Ulyett was not a particularly strong player, just a better batsman than most, presumably one of a number of enthusiastic if unskilled players. For example, Neale and Cobham took several wickets each - a statutory haul on bad wickets against weak batting, but seem to have been hit hard and often in the Caunton second innings; perhaps they tired too quickly. Fred Trueman is not keeping wicket, and his deputy did not cope very well. It is interesting that leg-byes are recorded after the Upton innings - an instance of the developments recording the scores.

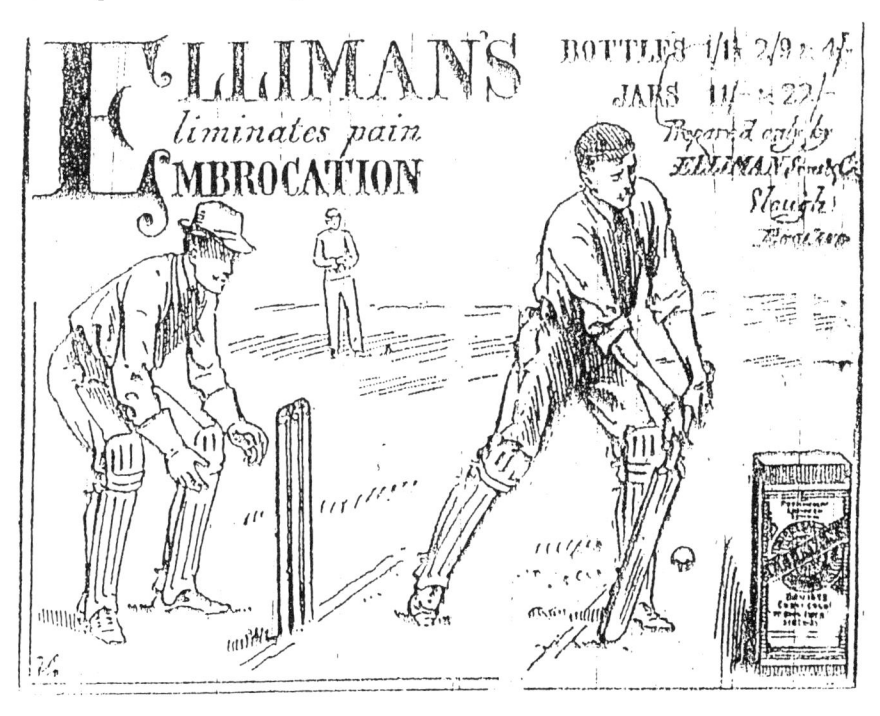

The next, third scorecard was not to appear until six years later, on August 12th, 1868. There had been very great drought and heat, which continued until the 21st of September. The harvest had begun on July 18th. The hay crops were very bad, and the wheat crop very large. A lawnmower might have been used to cut the grass for any of these three matches, for lawnmowers had been invented in 1830, almost by mistake. Edwin Budding, an engineer from Stroud, Gloucestershire, designed a machine to trim the excess material from wool cloth. He then realised that his cutting machine with cylindrical roller would also trim grass. The idea was not a great success until it was taken up by the Ipswich-based firm, Ransomes, in 1832, a company which still survives in the form of Ransome, Simms and Jefferies. Early mowers were used on sports grounds and large country houses. They were made of cast iron and so heavy that they had to be operated by two men. In 1841 Alexander Shanks of Arbroath built a large horse-drawn mower for a local landowner. The horse pulled, while a man on foot guided the machine. This is said to be the origin of the phrase "Shank's pony". Engines were not added until 1892, when the Leyland Steam Mower Company produced a steam mower. It weighed one and a half tons.

WINKBURN v UPTON - This match was played at Winkburn on Monday week and resulted in an easy victory for Winkburn.
Score:-

WINKBURN.

```
J Hallam, b Oldham................6    b Hatfield...................19
J Ridley, b Truman................1    b Hatfield....................2
J Asling, b Truman................0    b Truman.....................16
Mr A E Burnell, b Oldham.........10    c Morris, b Truman ..........4
Mr W A P Burnell, c Hatfield b Oldham.0 b Oldham....................16
J H Robinson,b Oldham.............1    c an b Truman................8
A Rickett, b Truman...............5    not out......................0
W M Jayes, lbw, b Oldham..........0    c Hatfield, b Truman.........0
T Payne, b Oldham.................4    c Cullen, b Horsley..........4
G Lowe, not out...................0    not out......................0
J Jepson, b Oldham................0    b Oldham.....................0
     Extras......................12         Extras.................16
         Total............39              Total..............96
```

UPTON.

```
G Rickett, b Asling...............2    b Hallam.....................3
R Hatfield,b A E Burnell..........4    b Asling.....................5
E Cullen, st E Burnell, b Hallam..6    b Asling.....................3
W Oldham,c Ridley, b Asling.......2    st A E Burnell b Asling......0
G Horsley, b Asling...............2    c Lowe b Asling..............0
L Morris, b Hallam................8    c W A P Burnell b Asling.....2
G Williams, l b w , b Hallam......2    b Asling.....................0
F Truman, run out.................1    st A E Burnell, b Hallam.....0
J Gill, st A E Burnell, b Hallam..0    b Asling.....................5
G Smith, c Ridley, b Hallam.......0    not out......................5
J Cooper, not out.................0    b Asling.....................2
     Extras.......................7         Extras..................2
         Total........................34              Total..............27
```

A dramatic change of personnel; not one of the side who played Caunton six years before remains. Two of the Winkburn players are of interest. Edward Burnell, aged 33, a lieutenant captain in the Coldstream Guards, was the eldest son of the Edward V. Pegg Burnell who was applied to for a donation when Upton were founded; he was also the president of the farming society, owner of Winkburn Hall, chairman of the Newark Magistrates, and a county magistrate. His second son had attended Eton and was aged 23. The Burnells lived in even greater style than the Falkners. To look after a family of five they employed a governess, a housekeeper, a cook, a ladies maid, a laundry maid, a house maid, a kitchen maid, a dairy maid, a butler, a page boy, a foot man, and two grooms. The Captain had his batman, Private Dickenson, living in the hall. Several other coachmen and bailiffs lived in tied accommodation, and there would have been a number of gardeners and farm labourers.

The Burnells profited by the coaching they had received; in each innings one of them makes a dominant score. The Upton bowling depended upon W. Oldham and Frederick Trueman with nine and seven wickets respectively, but, as in the Caunton match, they were unable to prevent a massive second innings total of ninety six, which seems to have demoralised Upton even further. Upton did not have bowling strength in depth; and without a Walter Whitaker the batting seems to have folded. It is interesting that Trueman, the experienced wicketkeeper, was once again called upon to bowl. His replacement behind the stumps again seems weak, for no stumpings were made, and 28 extras conceded. By contrast the younger Burnell made four stumpings and conceded only nine extras; but some of these nine could have been wides, and not his fault.

How would the teams have dressed? The majority of players would have made very little change to their clothes; boots, braces and belts, striped or dotted shirts would have been the rule. The Burnells and their friends, however, would have worn black "Oxford" cricket shoes, white trousers and shirts, floppy caps with short peaks, high collars and bow ties. The colours of Eton or the Coldstream Guards would have appeared on either pillbox hats or as ribbons around caps. Coloured shirts might have been worn, with spots, stripes, or checks.

The next match was reported on September 23rd, 1868.
UPTON v BALDERTON - *This match was played at Balderton on the 17th instant, and resulted in an easy victory for Upton in one innings.*

```
                            UPTON
Wade, c and b Richardson..............18    b Toulson...............2
J Hallam, c R Atter, b Richardson.....9     c bacon b Toulson.......0
Warriner, c Toulson, b Richardson.....2     run out.................5
G Rickett, run out....................27    c and b Toulson.........0
Cullen, run out.......................0     cRichardson bTowlson..18
J Elston, b Toulson...................5     b Richardson............8
J Gill, b Richardson..................0     c Daybell,b Richardson.0
G Parlby, c Richardson, b Toulson.....3     hit wicket..............1
T Payling, b Toulson..................6     b Richardson............8
J Cooper, b Toulson...................0     not out.................0
Mr Doubleday, not out.................2     run out.................7
     Byes 3, leg-bye 1................4         Byes................3
     Total..........................71         Total..............52
                          BALDERTON
Towlson, c and b Wade.................0     c Gill. b Wade..........3
Norledge. st Rickett, b Wade..........0     st Rickett, b Hallam...3
Richardson, c Warriner, b Wade.......12     b Hallam................5
J T Daybell, b Hallam.................3     c Wade, b Hallam........0
Walpole, st Rickett, b Hallam........10     run out.................2
```

```
G Atter. c Gill, b Wade................1      b Hallam................1
J Daybell, c Cullen, v Wade............1      b Hallam................2
Smithson, b Hallam.....................4      c Elston, b Hallam.....0
R Atter, c Rickett, b Hallam ..........0      not out.................3
Wright, c Warriner, b Wade.............1      st Rickett, b Hallam...2
Bacon, not out.........................0      c Payling, b Wade......3
    Byes 4, leg-bye 1..................5          Wide................1
    Total.........................40              Total...........25
```

A convincing win for Upton. J. Hallam, who had played for Winkburn six weeks before against Upton, now opens the batting for Upton. This reflects the friendship between Upton and Winkburn which persists to the present day. The Reverend Naylor had specifically written in his prospectus that the team should be open to the neighbourhood. Rickett, Cullen, Gill and Cooper also play again, and in similar order. This time Rickett plays the innings of the day to steer Upton to a dominating total; none of the other survivors contribute very much. Wade takes eight wickets for Upton, and Hallam takes eleven, to add to the six he had taken against Upton previously. Once again a Mr. Doubleday appears in the side, probably the original steward. Once again we see a side collapsing totally in their fourth innings, obviously feeling that 84 runs was an unreachable goal. We have evidence, therefore, that Upton had a pool of players, and that Rickett is probably the reserve wicket keeper when Trueman is not available or has to bowl. He seems to have improved a great deal in six weeks, and only permits one bye while making two stumpings. This might be a reflection on the wickets; the ground at Winkburn where he had a bad match is poor and uneven to this day, for the modern club sees itself as a genial collection of farmers who play cricket when other activities permit - it fits in with the seasonal round of farming, shooting, hunting, and so on, and there are not enough hours in the day for the nuances of groundsmanship.

In conclusion, the club seems to have suffered from the loss of the Whitakers. No strong core of players appears to have developed. Only two of the original stewards are still involved after thirteen years. The scores are rather low. One feels that the strong and forceful influence of The Reverend Naylor exercised has been missed.

Chapter six
A School to be Proud Of

Upton School was founded by the Collies Charity in 1826. It joined the National Society in 1863, and was hence forward known as "The National School", but it is interesting that Upton, like many another village, had some kind of school 44 years before the Education Act of 1870 made education compulsory for all children. There are about a dozen references to the school in the "Advertiser's" columns, nearly all revealing achievements and progress. In March 1880 the Diocesan School Inspector, the Rev. R.H. Whitworth, spoke about the *'advantages of a good circulating library ... and also addressed a few words to parents on the punctuality and regularity of their children at school'*. Diocesan inspectors are usually the most mild and affable of creatures, in no way to be confused with those from a local education authority, so there must have been some reason for disquiet. Perhaps the levels of absenteeism were high when harvests needed to be got in, and every pair of hands was needed in the fields. This could be a massive source of friction in farming communities.

However, just before Christmas all was sweetness and light when an entertainment was held to raise funds for a harmonium for the schoolroom. Obviously a piano was not good enough; a harmonium is a reed-organ, the air being forced or drawn through reeds, to produce a sound not unlike an organ in a church. It also a hitherto unreported willingness to raise funds for the education of their own children rather than for charities. *'The children sang "Withered leaves" in a style which reflected great credit on themselves and their master, Mr. Fisher'* and the usual performers obliged with songs, solos, duets, and readings.

Mr. Fisher moved on, and was succeeded by Mr. Willis, who seems to have won the affection and respect of both pupils and parents. On the last day of October, 1884, we find him conducting the children during a fine entertainment for the Prize Fund; Miss Peacock, the vicar's daughter was playing the new harmonium. Three weeks later there was evidence that the village's boys were succeeding in high education. One of the sons of Professor Branford, a former resident, had won two bursaries and a gold medal at Edinburgh University. Mr. Willis's energy is obvious; before the winter was over, another entertainment was given during the annual prize-giving. There had been but one failure in the core subjects of English and mathematics. Mr. Willis ended the proceedings with a solo. He sang again, in the company of the usual musicians, in another fund-raising concert for the school the following November. But good teachers are difficult to keep, and the following July, 1886, he left Upton, after three years, for the larger school at Laxton. He and his wife were presented with an album, a butter dish, and several other presents "of a private nature". His successor seems to have found the pupils to his liking, for praise was won from the Rev. C. Sewell, an HMI, after an inspection on May 23rd, 1888.

'With some exception for the work of the Fourth Standard, all the exercises were very well done indeed. The musical exercises warrant the higher grant ...'.

The merit grant is excellent, and the highest amount of grant yet earned by the school has been received. There were seven classes; infant, and standards one to six. The following year the visiting HMI was Mr. Webster, and the report is equally good.

'The standard work was done in a most creditable way throughout the school. Class work was unequal, but except for want of intelligence in the girls' recitation of standard three, it was good. Order and singing are particularly pleasing, but the ear exercises were rather imperfect. The infants are well taught'.

The excellent merit grant was earned with a grant of 20s. 7d. per scholar in average attendance.

In 1895 and 1896 there is further evidence of a good school. On the 23rd of April if was examined in drawing and awarded "excellent" by the Department of Science and Art. But there was even better news the following June, especially for a teacher faced with an annual inspection.

'..In place of the annual examination, these schools have this year been inspected under Article 84b of the code. Her Majesty's Inspector has paid two visits without notice during the past school year, each visit lasting the whole of the school meeting. The highest grants have again been earned in both mixed and infant departments, and the report states that "Excellent work is done, and the children are attentive and diligent. The condition of the upper department is most creditable". My Lords have sanctioned the omission of the annual examination due in May, 1897. At the drawing exam held under the Science and Art Department in March last, this school again gained the award excellent......'

In April 1898 there was an extensive musical programme by the children of all ages in aid of the scholar's prize fund. Once again the question of regular and punctual attendance was raised in the chairman's opening remarks.

> *'Where everything went so well, it is very difficult to particularise, but special mention must be made of the Five Infants in the "Dolly" song, which fairly brought down the house, and the droll way in which the little mites (John Moss, Frank Stimson, and Annie Carby) got through their recitations was a treat ...'*

Mr. and Mrs. Lawley, the master and mistress, were warmly thanked at the end for the pains they had taken".

Annie Carby was one of sixteen children of John Carby, who worked on the short-lived railway at Southwell. The family lived next to "The Little Shop". Less than ninety years later the school would also close when the roll fell below thirty, although the closure was bitterly resisted by parents and past pupils. This meant that there was a very fine building suitable for conversion into a family home, and fittingly enough it was one of Annie Carby's great-nephews, John Carby, who saw the possibilities.

Chapter seven
Nineteen Terrible Years
After the report of the Winkburn match in August, 1868, nearly eleven years were to pass until another appeared. In July 1879 Upton beat Rolleston by eight wickets. The following year they lost to Newark Hartington and Newark Castle; in 1883 they lost to a Farnsfield XI at Farnsfield, and in 1884 they lost at home to Fiskerton, then to Averham. All this contrasts strongly with the good defensive work of a local boy in the Zulu wars! Gonville Bromhead, late of the Magnus School, won the Victoria Cross. He was in command at Rorke's Drift, an old mission station, and defended it successfully against hordes of Zulus immediately after the English field force to which his detachment belonged had been wiped out at Islanwhana.

While the Upton team seemed to have slipped into something approaching terminal decline, cricket had seen momentous events and improvements. In 1870 a heavy roller was used at Lord's for the first time; at last the batsmen in the first-class game found pitches they could trust. The benefit was seen immediately. W.G. Grace had his best ever year in 1871, scoring 2,739 runs at an average of over 78. His scores included 189 not out, 268 and 217. In 1872 Lord's experimented with covering the pitch before the start of a match; this would mean that the batsman would not have to cope with rain-damaged wickets, which had given enormous assistance to the bowler. Unsurprisingly, in 1876 Grace established two more records;
  (1) the first score of over 300 in a first class match - 344 for MCC versus Kent at Canterbury. His next two scores for Gloucestershire were 127 versus Nottinghamshire and 318 versus Yorkshire.
  (2) 400 not out for an All-England XI against XI v. XXII of Grimsby.

Momentously, in 1877 England played the first test match against Australia at Melbourne, and in 1878 Australia toured England and beat a strong MCC side in a single day.

The Rolleston match of 1879 is of more than usual interest because it is the very first evidence of a cricket match being played at Upton. The fact that it was against Rolleston, whose scorecards were printed frequently, suggests that once again Upton were indebted to "the other side" for sending the scorecard to the Advertiser. It would be pleasant to report an improvement in the Upton performance, but the truth is that there had been too much change in one sense, and not enough in another. Not one Upton player had ever played for the village before, as far as we know; there was a complete lack of continuity since the match at Balderton 11 years before. Fred Trueman, who had probably been a mainstay of the club since 1855, would have been 46, and had probably given up the game. The batting on both sides was hopelessly weak - in thirty three innings, only three batsmen reach double figures, and fifteen failed to score; three batsmen registered "pairs"; they failed to score in either innings. More tellingly, half of the wickets that fell were clean bowled. The familiar pattern of nineteenth century village cricket is seen again; the life expectancy of batsmen with no defensive technique facing competent bowling on dreadful wickets is all too short. But in fairness to the batsmen of both sides, it is unlikely that a even a light roller had been used in the preparation of the wicket. Upton made do with a light roller until 1990, and this latest roller is by no means of the heaviest.

ROLLESTON V UPTON - Played at Upton July 8th.

ROLLESTON

W. Marshall. c and b Fisher	11	b Hadfield	0
J. Rochford, b Cooling	2	b Fisher	2
T. Cullen, c Hadfield b Cooling	1	c and b Fisher	10
A. Sharpe, run out	0	b Fisher	0
J. Bedford, c J Cox, b Cooling	3	b Fisher	0
E. Crowder, c Fisher, b Cooling	0	run out	0
T. Payling, not out	2	b Fisher	0
W. Lewis, b Cooling	4	b Fisher	1
C. Blyton, b Fisher	4	b Fisher	2
W. Sheppard, cF.Foster,b Cooling	2	c and b Fisher	2
W. Pepper, b Fisher	0	not out	0
Extras	2	Extras	2
Total	31	Total	17

UPTON

S. Foster, b Marshall	3	not out	11
F. Keyworth, b Crowder	2	b Cullen	0
J. Hadfield, b Marshall	2	not out	7
F. Fisher, b Crowder	0		
J. Parlby, c Sheppard, b Crowder	0		
A. Cooling, b Crowder	0		
J. Cox, st Cullen, b Crowder	0		
J. Aldridge. not out	5	c Blyton, b Cullen	3
T. Cox, c Blyton, b Crowder	6		
F. Foster, run out	0		
H. Hardington, b Marshall	1		
Extras	5	Extra	1
Total	31	Total	22

So Upton won by 8 wickets. On the plus side, Fisher took eleven wickets for them, but again one emphasises that is the least a decent bowler would expect in the circumstances.

On Saturday, 12th of June, 1880, Upton played a two innings game against Newark Hartington, in Newark. Hartington scored 116, Upton 65. Only one Upton batsman reached double figures - A. Salt made 14.

On Wednesday October 16th - it must have been a pleasant autumn - Upton played Newark Castle on the field by the Sconce on the road to Farndon. It is now the Sconce Hills recreation ground. Once again Mr. Salt got into double figures - 20 - but the other eight made only 31 between them; sadly, two of the Upton side had failed to turn up. Despite fine bowling by Salt, who took five wickets, and F. Fisher, who took the other five, Castle made 57 in their only innings and won by an innings and six runs.

Nearly three years later we have a report of a match at Farnsfield. The fact that they fielded "an eleven" suggests that they were in no doubt about their own strengths or Upton's probable weaknesses, a clairvoyance which is supported by the result. Upton were beaten by eight wickets; they batted first and were dismissed for twelve, six batsman failing to score, among them Mr. Willis, the much respected teacher at the village school who batted at number eleven. Farnsfield then made 69, but they were up against at least two Upton bowlers of ability in William Sheppard and T. Curzon. William Sheppard was aged 23. The son of the village grocer, he had set up his own carrier's business. He gradually learned to bat and bowl, and in this, the second match that we know he played, took two wickets. So did Curzon, who was 21, and lived with his mother, who was on parish relief. Two more were taken by a man named Potter, who also held a catch. Potter then scored 21 in Upton's reply 62, which left Farnsfield to score only six to win. Potter never played for Upton again; having been run out in the first innings, top scored in the second, taken two wickets and held a catch, and ending up on the losing side, he probably decided to look for stronger support elsewhere.

On Saturday, July 12th, 1884, Upton entertained Fiskerton, and went down by six wickets. Fragile batting meant that Upton only scored 46 and 45. Fiskerton replied with 59 and 39 for 4. However, William Sheppard's elder brother Tom, aged 29, batted well in both innings for 23 runs. Mr. Willis the schoolteacher was his partner in a stand that shored up the Upton first innings.

On Thursday 9th July, 1885, Averham were entertained at home. They won by nine wickets. In a two innings match Robert Samuel Foster, the village baker, who lived at the Hollies at the corner of Church Lane, made 41 of Upton's total of 79. Averham replied with 38 and 73 for five, and probably won by nine wickets. Foster also took three wickets, and William Sheppard the carrier bowled well, as ever, but it was not enough, for the Upton card included twelve ducks.

So ended possibly the worst era in the history of cricket in Upton. It is obvious that there were one or two useful players among a majority who had but a casual interest in the game, but a strong central core of good players were needed. This was not to appear until 1887.

Chapter eight
Jubilees and Fun

Within ten years there were three occasions when there was an excuse to push the parishional boat out in the grandest ways possible, and the opportunities were taken by every parish in the county. The rejoicings in Upton were similar to those reported in other parishes, although Kirklingon found the money to hire the Southwell Silver Band. June 29th, 1887, marked the fiftieth anniversary of Queen Victoria's accession to the throne.

'The Queen's Jubilee was celebrated with great enthusiasm in this village. The proceedings began at an early hour. At nine o'clock all the children, with many of their parents and friends, assembled in Mr Falkner's grounds to partake of frumenty, which had been kindly prepared for the occasion from ingredients supplied for the most part gratuitously by various friends. This form of treat was suggested and largely promoted by an inhabitant who had not forgotten the gratification which he had received as a boy from a similar treat on the Queen's accession. About eleven o'clock the children of the Church and Wesleyan Sunday Schools met in the National School-room to receive Jubilee medals. They afterwards marched in procession, accompanied by their teachers, to the church, where a short service with an address from the vicar was held. There was a large congregation. Service over, the men and youths of sixteen years of age and above, gathered in full force in Mr. Cottingham's grounds, and in a shed, very kindly lent for the occasion, sat down to a hot dinner of excellent beef and mutton and new potatoes, all capitally dressed. Dinner ended, the vicar proposed the Queen's health in an appropriate speech, and hearty, ringing cheers were given for her Majesty. At four o'clock the children were entertained at a meat tea. At five the women were similarly provided for, and were joined at tea by the men, who were beginning to recover their appetites. Tea over, cricket and other games were the order of the day. Later on a supper followed of bread and Stilton cheese and beer for the men, and of cake and temperance drinks for the women. Thus ended a very happy day. Great satisfaction was expressed by all at the excellent arrangements of the committee, and so ample was the provision made that enough was left over to divide next day amongst twenty-five of the poorer families of the place.'

One of the reasons for the youths' recovery of appetite was that some of them had spent much of the day bathing in the River Greet near the race-course; thus Walter Trueman told the Reverend West sixty years later.

> GENTLEMEN.
>
> COATS.
> TROUSERS.
> SUITS
> OVERCOATS.
> TENNIS OUTFITS
>
> PATROL SUITS, from 2s.11d.
> SAILOR SUITS from 4s.6d
> JERSEY SUITS, from 2s.11d.
> NORFOLK SUITS. from 8s.6d.
> JACK TAR SUITS, 8s.6d.

Six years later the Prince of Wales, the future King Edward the seventh, married. Some of the villagers would probably see him before his death in 1910, for he was often a guest of the Savilles at Rufford Abbey during Doncaster Races. He enjoyed motoring from Rufford to Doncaster in a procession of Rolls-Royces.

While the happy event was being celebrated throughout the length and breadth of the land on Thursday last, the quiet and pleasant little village of Upton was not entirely behind the scenes. The colours which were displayed in various parts of the village considerably added to the gaiety of its appearance. In the afternoon all the children attending the Day and Sunday Schools assembled at the National School. They were there marshalled, and bearing banners and accompanied by their teachers, proceeded to the Sunday Schoolroom, which was tastefully decorated for the occasion. Here they did most ample justice to the excellent tea provided for them. The children's tea was followed by another for adults, and to which 180 sat down at six p.m. All afterwards repaired to a field kindly lent for the purpose, when the children indulged in various games, scrambling for nuts, sweets, etc.

Only four years later the Queen provided her people for yet another reason for celebration, the sixtieth anniversary of her accession, in June 1897.

The festivities in connection with the commemoration of the Queen's reign commenced at Upton on Tuesday. At eleven o'clock there was a parade of the Upton Independent Friendly Society in their full regalia and the school children, who looked very gay, as each one carried either a flag or flowers. On arriving at the church there was a short service, conducted by the Vicar. After the service the male section of the age of sixteen and upwards proceeded to the French Horn Club-room,where, at one o'clock, they sat down to a splendid dinner, which consisted of roast beef and plum pudding. The Rev. W.J. Peacocke presided, and during the course of the proceedings proposed the health of the Queen, which was most enthusiastically drunk, three cheers being also given for her Majesty. A delightful programme of music was provided and this was greatly enjoyed by those present, the performers consisting of a string band from Nottingham. At half-past three the children sat down to tea in the Sunday School-room, where each child was presented with a jubilee mug. At five o'clock a meat tea was provided for the female sex of sixteen and upwards in the above room, which was crowded. For their refreshment there was a plentiful supply of beef, ham, plum cake, bread and butter, etc. The tables were tastefully decorated with flowers, and everything passed off most successfully. The band was in attendance, and again contributed to the harmony of the occasion. At six o'clock the men were provided with a substantial tea. During the afternoon a cricket match was played between a picked eleven and twenty-two, which resulted in a win for the former. The evening was spent in games and sports, dancing being freely indulged in to the strains of the band. There was a plentiful supply of John Barleycorn, aerated waters, and tobacco for the seniors, whilst the youngsters were amused in scrambling for nuts and sweets. The band, at the conclusion of the days festivities, played the National Anthem, which was heartily sung by those present. So ample were the supplies, the festivities were continued on Thursday evening, when there was a supper provided for men in the club room, after which the evening was spent singing patriotic and other songs. On Friday evening the women sat down to a meat tea, after which the children were similarly entertained. The evening was again spent in games and dancing, the music being provided by local players. The village was prettily decorated with garlands, flags, mottoes,

&. *The expenses were defrayed by public subscription, and the field for sports, &., was kindly lent by Mr. Knight.*

Upton normally had a feast day on about the second Thursday in July, and this article gives a very good idea how it was spent, if allowance is made for the rather silly style of the report.

'THE FEAST AND DONKEY RACES. *On Thursday last the "Saracen's Head Hotel", Southwell, was the rendezvous of the sporting fraternity residing in the town and neighbourhood. Postilions in their blue jackets with gilt buttons and gold-laced caps were strutting about the streets in all directions. Your humble correspondent, always anxious to know what is going on, made enquiries of one of the post boys, and ascertaining that it was Upton donkey races, I politely asked a friends of mine, who is familiarly known by the name of "The Shah", to drive me to the long straggling village which is situated about two miles from Southwell; and at six o'clock in the evening away we went in postilion style, with waggonette, the crowds in the street cheering us as we went down Church St. at a rattling pace with Horsley's best pair of steeds. On our arrival at Upton we drove into the yard belonging to Mr. Milward, a thorough old English gentleman; and alighting were ushered into his hospitable parlour, where we found the magnates of the locality enjoying themselves to their hearts' content. Shortly after our arrival we proceeded to the race ground, a field kindly lent for the occasion by Mr. Collingham. There were hundreds of people of both sexes assembled on the course at the time of the first event on the list taking place, which was the "Donkeyster" Stakes for Jehus of all ages; and on the signal being given for the start, six of the rough-coated quadrupeds made their appearance at the post. Mr. John Milward officiated as the starter, and Mr. Samuel Horsley as judge. After a short delay, off they started, some one way and some the other, and, like pigs, anyway but the right one. After a deal of coaxing and whipping, the jockeys got them into something like proper racing form, but, as the old saying is, "There's many a slip 'twixt the cup and the lip", so it was with the unfortunate riders, some of their steeds on reaching the turning flag lay down with their burdens underneath them, others knelt down and pitched the inexperienced riders over their heads, throwing a complete somersault in the air, and coming down on the green sward with a dull thud. After a long time the winning post was reached, and Mr. Cooling's animal declared the winner of the first prize, and Mr. Straton's the second. The next event was a woman's race, for which seven prizes were offered, but the efforts*

of it doing anything unnatural. The outcome was plenty of attractive shots played with the full swing of the bat. Unquestionably, cricket was a less complicated game, but it must have been enormous fun to play and watch. There was also the enthusiasm and dedication of the huge crowds, and the adulation accorded the popular cricketing heroes, whose status was so much less challenged by other distractions. The game was played with great seriousness yet also with true "joie de vivre". The great batsmen illuminated cricket grounds with their elegantly impassive strokeplay, but without thought for entertainment; it was the spontaneous expression of their love of cricket and delight in hitting the ball.

From the embers of the golden age came famous amateur captains of England; Douglas Jardine, and later Peter May, Mike Smith and Colin Cowdrey, all from similar backgrounds. Colin Cowdrey is a perfect example of the breed; brought up in the tropics, coached every day from the age of five, education and more coaching in independent schools by cricket-mad masters, and finishing at Oxford or Cambridge, where the young master batsman was honed to perfection by large staffs of wily old professional cricketers. When his university summer term ended in June, Colin packed his kit and moved to the Kent county ground at Canterbury, where some luckless professional was dropped to make room for him.

Upton's first, infinitely more modest golden age began in 1887. We have records of four matches played in that year; against Kelham (lost by 21 runs), Halam (won by 64 runs), and Kelham and Averham twice (lost by an innings and 44 runs, won by 24 runs). Kelham and Averham had amalgamated in either August or September of that year. The results and scores are unimportant - Upton's highest total in six innings was 86; what was significant was that a nucleus of six players played in three of those games, and therefore probably throughout the season - J. Cottingham, Robert Samuel Foster, Thomas Hadfield, F.O.N. Peacocke, W. Pollitt, and William Shepherd. But much more significantly, Walter Trueman, old Frederick's oldest son, played against Halam on August 1st. He was now aged 21. His Jubilee celebrations four weeks before - a dip in the Greet, beef and mutton lunch, meat tea with the ladies, and a hefty supper of Stilton - had done him good, and somehow opened his eyes to the game of games. The other two sons were rather young for the hurly-burly of the game at a man's level. Ernest Trueman was only 16, and Henry ("Harry") only 12. Old Fred had probably not played for perhaps twenty years, but he must have relished the thought that at last he could see his own sons in action. There had been bad results and disappointing times. Now he could pass on the torch, see what his own flesh and blood could do to gain revenge. Would these three strapping young sons with brick layers hands and muscles take to the game? Fred was confident they would; surely it was he who sent the reports to the Advertiser, raising the profile of his village team for domestic reasons? Or was he performing some subconscious process of atonement to the soul of the long-dead Reverend Naylor, for not producing a worthwhile team sooner?

In 1888 we have records of four more matches; against Halam (won by 8 wickets), Maythorne Lace Mills (won by an innings and 18 runs), F. Parker's XI (won by an innings and 20 runs), and Laxton (won by 31 runs). In terms of the low scoring matches of the time, these are crushing victories, and suggest a very successful season indeed. We can see that ten players - A.H. Bickley, J. Cobham, T. Cox, W. Esam, Robert Samuel Foster, W. Foster, Thomas Hadfield, R. Marshall, William Sheppard, and Walter Trueman all played regularly. Bickley was a good opening bat who bowled well, Esam a middle order bat and a good fast bowler, and Sheppard an experienced all-rounder and a good clubman. The reports say that the Upton fielding was excellent. But one match report intrigues and excites the cricket historian more than any of the other thirty available to us.

Saturday, July 23rd, 1888.
UPTON v LAXTON These teams met at Laxton on Saturday. The game resulted in an easy win for Upton, none of the Laxton team being able to stand up against the bowling of Esam and Jackson.....

Jackson took four wickets in the first innings, and five in the second. Could this be John Jackson again, the terror of England and the world's fastest bowler thirty years before? We know that he was alive in the eighteen nineties. What reasons are there for supposing he was playing for Upton at Laxton? There are three; the obvious fast bowling ability shown, his association with Upton through the longstanding friendship with the Whitaker family, and the fact that Laxton is only about four miles from Wellow, where we know that Jackson lived at the height of his fame. Against this one might protest that the man would have been in his sixties. But age, although it removes a great player's genius, often leaves a substantial residue of the highest ability, until infirmity removes him from the field completely. Wilfred Rhodes bowled for England when he was 52.

Maybe Jackson's fast bowler's frame allowed him to play the odd game of village cricket until very late in his life.

In 1889 only one scorecard, was printed, a home game versus Newark Builders, who were flattened by the bowling of Bickley and Sheppard, who shared nine wickets. Walter, Ernest, and Harry Trueman all played in this match, only Ernest troubling the scorer. No builder reaches double figures in their score of 23; Upton might also have fared badly had not Bickley made 12 batting at number 3. As it was they made 47. The builders were allowed a second innings, and in this Walter and Harry both took wickets. Harry would then have been aged 15.

In 1890 we have records of five matches against other villages, and two games which show how the nature of the game was altering. There were two games against Muskham in May and June; they won by 7 runs at home, and lost 6 wickets at Muskham. In July they lost to H.W. Walker's XI at Averham by 10 runs. H.W. Walker was the vicar of Averham, a formidable bowler, and probably the patron of the Kelham and Averham team, whose ground adjoined his rectory. In August they beat Kirklington at home by 29 runs, and 61 runs at Kirklington. Also in that month came the first "village game", where the club challenged twenty-two other players. The club made 100 for 7 wickets the first recorded instance of them reaching three figures - while the twenty-two hopefuls amassed 51 in two innings. We can see in this game the gap that had opened up between those who played regularly and obviously were working at their game, and those who would turn out for an afternoon in their work boots and braces if asked. Sheppard took eight of the first ten wickets for less than eight runs, when presumably he was asked by his captain to have a rest until the second innings, where he took three more before time ran out. Ernest Trueman claimed six stumpings and Harry took about six wickets, and then there was another "Twenty-two match." The last game of the season was another village game; Harry and Walter were obviously disappointed that October was nearly on them, and raised a side each. Harry's team appears to be the nearly the village side; he batted at number three, and made 20 of his side's total of 39. He helped Sheppard dismiss Walter's side for 37, taking two wickets while Sheppard took five.

Thus ended 1890, a significant and pivotal year for the club. They had played against a representative side, smashed a twenty-two, and shown they had the reserves and enthusiasm to play far into the Autumn.

UPTON C.C. ELEVEN v. TWENTY-TWO.—Played at Upton on Saturday last. Score:—

THE TWENTY-TWO.	
J Stimson, c E Trueman, b Pariby	1
F Trueman, b Pariby	0
T Martin, b Pariby	1
A Watts, b Pariby	6
J Gill, b Pariby	5
W Cooper, b Sheppard	3
J Williams, b Sheppard	0
D Marsh, b Pariby	0
H Brown, b Sheppard	0
F Keyworth, b Pariby	0
G Launders, b W Trueman	0
W Launders, b Pariby	0
T Curzon, b W Trueman	2
S Kent, b Halliday	10
G Smith, not out	3
T Foster, c and b Halliday	2
T Ironmonger, b Halliday	3
G Williams, c T. Sheppard, b Mathers	0
F Rickett, b W. Trueman	2
T Watts, b Pariby	1
J Sumner, b Halliday	4
T Trueman, b Halliday	11
Extras	4
	62

THE ELEVEN.	
E Trueman, b F Trueman	0
H Trueman, b F Keyworth, b F Trueman	11
W Sheppard, b Gill	50
W Mathers, c Watts, b Launders	3
W Trueman, c and b Gill	18
T Sheppard, not out	15
T Cox, b Gill	1
H Savage, b Gill	1
J Pariby, c Gill	1
Extras	2
	87

H G Halliday did not bat.

Old Fred's three sons were producing match winning performances. T. Cox, W. Dixon, the schoolteacher H.G. Halliday, C. and H. Lidgett, W. Mathers, A. Mills, J.R. and T. Parlby, William Sheppard, and W. Wollatt had played regularly and well, but the three older Trueman brothers hadn't missed a match between them; they obviously lived for the game.

UPTON C.C. v. UPTON VILLAGE.—This match was played on Saturday between the newly-organised club and a team chosen from the village, which consisted chiefly of veterans, with the exception of one or two younger players. For the village F. Trueman played capitally for 32, whilst Dodson, Suter, Marsh, and Woollatt, made useful scores, the latter veteran carried out his bat in the second venture after showing a stubborn defence, and defying several changes of bowlers. For the team representing the club, it is only fair to state that they are composed chiefly of juniors, the match under notice being the first the majority of them had taken part in, and it was pleasing to notice that several of the juniors showed very promising form, both with bat and ball, and deserve great credit for the plucky stand they made against the elder players, the chief contributors being P. Cox, H. Rawson, P. Marsh, G. Beckett, T. Marsh, and J. Brown, the latter also bowled splendidly throughout both innings, whilst G. Beckett performed well behind the stumps, as will be seen by the small score of extras. After the match the players adjourned to the Rein Deer Inn pavilion, where they were met by a large number of friends, and sat down to a splendid supper, provided by Host and Hostess Rawson, after which the remainder of the evening was spent in harmony. Score:—

UPTON C.C.

J Brown, c Woollatt, b Sheppard	0	b F Trueman	5
S Marsh, b W Trueman	7	b Marsh	2
G Parlby, b W Trueman	0	b Marsh	1
G Beckett, c Dodson, b Sheppard	5	b F Trueman	2
G Sheppard, b W Trueman	2	b Marsh	2
E Rawson, c&b W Trueman	0	b F Trueman	1
O Wood, c Dodson, b Sheppard	0	c J Cox, b Marsh	3
T Marsh, b Sheppard	0	not out	7
P Cox, b Sheppard	9	b Marsh	7
H Rawson, not out	8	c and b Marsh	1
P Pritchett, st Sheppard, b F Trueman	0	c J Cox, b Trueman	1
H Ellis, b F Trueman	5	b Marsh	7
Extras	2	Extras	4
	38		43

UPTON VILLAGE.

T Dodson, b Brown	6	c Ellis, b Brown	3
J Rawson, b Brown	0	b Brown	1
W Sheppard, b Brown	10	b Brown	14
F Trueman, c and b Ellis	32	c Ellis, b Parlby	8
W Trueman, run out	2	b Ellis	2
T Cox, c and b S Marsh	3	b Brown	2
H Dayman, b S Marsh	0	b Brown	2
T Suter, b Brown	6	run out	0
P Marsh, b Ellis	1	b Brown	8
J Woollatt, run out	1	not out	6
J Lawson, not out	1	st Beckett, b Ellis	0
J Cox, c H Rawson, b Brown	1	b Ellis	5
Extras	1	Extras	4
	64		55

64

The first match printed in 1891, was Upton C.C. v a Twenty-Two on July 9th - Feast Thursday. The Upton side is picked on unsentimental grounds; young Frederick, aged 14, has to play for the Twenty-Two while his three big brothers play for the club. The Twenty-Two were beaten, 44-41. The gulf between the two different types of player is not so obvious this time; only one player gets into double figures - Ernest Trueman scores 20, and young Frederick took two wickets. A week later they went to Kelham and were soundly thrashed; Kelham and Averham made 86, Harry taking two wickets. Upton were given two innings and made only 36 runs. The reason for the humiliation of the Upton team was the bowling for Averham of the Reverend H.W. Walker, who took 11 of the 16 wickets that fell for 16 runs; but Upton had fallen from grace slightly, by turning up with only nine men. The third match was on the 15th of August - another Club versus Twenty-Two; the club won by 25 runs, 87-62. Finally, in September they played Muskham at Muskham; Upton had learnt by bitter experience, and had asked the Reverend Walker to play for them. The match appeared to end in a tie, with the scores level at 56. Upton were deemed winners as they had three wickets in hand. H.W.Walker took seven wickets at a very low cost. This clergyman must have been a prime example of the wealthy amateur who did so much for cricket in these years, and typified the spirit of the golden age that would dawn in 1900. He had a wide range of interests, because we know that he kept a hunter and a groom, Mr. Hannaford, to look after it. Later he was to take a significant part in the creation of the Robin Hood theatre. His photograph, lying on the ground in the middle of the Averham team, shows a man with a sense of humour, too.

At this fascinating point the trail goes very cold, for not another Upton match was printed until 1900. Old Fred died in 1892, which might account for this. The only 1900 scorecard we have shows Upton C.C. versus Upton Village: *'the newly organised club and a team chosen from the village... For the team representing the club, it is only fair to state that they are composed chiefly of juniors, the match under notice being the first the majority had taken part in...'* Fred and Walter are not playing for this new young side, but for the opposition. The powers-that-were would have recognised that Harry's commitments were to his paymasters, and Walter's were to Averham. It was the village's loss. Either of them would have been good captains. Both were young; Fred 23, and Walter 34. Harry made 32 in the first innings, and Bill Shephard made 10; no-one else reached double figures all day.

Mr. Warwick, the brewer who had bought Upton Hall, was now president. We know that the Trueman's allegiances had switched towards Averham to an extent. One suspects that "H.W." Wilfred Walker had taken an interest in Harry, and told him that there was a future in the game for him. Anyway, Averham were a better side, and their wickets were probably better prepared. Whatever the reasons, we know that Harry and Ernest played for them throughout the 'nineties. In 1896 we see that they played Rolleston and made 288, of which Harry made 77. A few days later they made 209-5 against Ossington, who replied with 32. These are massive scores in the context of the time, and can only confirm that Wilfred Walker had assembled and coached some kind of super team that had the luxury of a flat surface to play on. In 1897, 1898, and 1899 the Truemans turned out for them again; in one match Winthorpe were beaten 107-9. In 1900 Harry played for them on May 16th, and there is a note that *"Tea was provided by the vicar"*. We know that Harry had turned professional sometime in the eighteen nineties; the most likely scenario is that Walker had helped him in this, and in return Fred would play the occasional match for them when he was available. We know that he was a professional for Burleigh Park, and won a medal by taking one hundred wickets for Mansfield in 1900, so it may well be that he was paid to play for Averham and Kelham occasionally.

We may conjecture that the Upton club had suffered through the loss of two of their keenest players, and the death of old Fred. There could have been difficulties until Mr. Warwick, who loved the game, and who had bought Upton Hall, injected cash and enthusiasm and business expertise, and saw the need for a fresh start and a team of youngsters.

Chapter ten
Emigration

Many villagers had gone; some to the factories and mills, others to Australia or America. A series of reports and advertisements in the Advertiser show that very considerable efforts were being made by a least one American railway company to attract farm labourers to its country. Thus, November 8th, 1871:

'EMIGRATION TO IOWA AND NEBRASKA. The third edition of "The Emigrant's guide to Iowa and Nebraska" is worth the careful attention of all who are intending to seek a home in the Western World. It is not necessary to reiterate the facts regarding the formation of the Burlington and Missouri-River Railroad by an enterprising and wealthy company, to whom the United States Government made a grant of nearly two million acres of land. That railway having been formed, the company have every possible interest in securing the comfortable settlement of emigrant families on the land along the route, and to accomplish that object they are expending large sums of money, and offering terms more advantageous that have ever before been presented to the agricultural population of this country, to induce them to try their fortune abroad instead of leading a life of hopeless toil at home. A colony will leave England about March, 1872, to join the three colonies that left in 1871, and will be accompanied from Liverpool to their destination by an officer of the company. Those wishing to join should apply early to any of the company's agents, or at their offices. The party will be conveyed in a special train direct from their port of landing to their destination. A number of encouraging letters have been received by the company's officers in England, from settlers who have gone out to Nebraska during the present year....'

Three glowing accounts of life in Nebraska follow, including this one from the financial manager of the company:

'...Mr. Hatcliffe and his family, who went with our second colony (booked by you), is comfortably settled near the new city of Lincoln, having been put on a farm of 100 acres to farm the land on shares - i.e. for his labour to receive half the value of the products of the land. Mr. Hatcliffe had 26 years experience as a farm labourer near Horncastle, and is now able to make a comfortable living, and will soon be, I doubt not, not only a farmer, but a landed proprietor.'

It is the sort of letter that a sales manager would write. However, there are two accompanying letters, one from a West Bromwich man, which radiate similar enthusiasm.

Only three weeks later there was another article, this time respecting a talk that the Rev. J.B. Kaye gave in the "Balderton school rooms"; he was going to form a colony in Minnesota.

'...He gave a glowing description of the country, its fertility, timber, and water; the high wages given to labourers, being double as much as in England; that although the climate was cold ... He gave great encouragement to the emigration of small farmers with large families, as also to blacksmiths, carpenters, & who were not able, through want of capital, to make their way in England ... He appeared to give great satisfaction to a very numerous audience.'

"Although the climate was cold.." is euphemistic. The winters are bitterly cold, with blizzards. Houses may be buried for weeks and farms snowbound for months. This next advertisement appeared in following June (it is always best to cross the Atlantic during the summer months, though very bad weather is possible).

"Send for the Emigrants guide to Iowa and Nebraska. Issued free, by post one penny; containing particulars of PRAIRIE FARMS AND GOOD LANDS for sale at low prices GIVING TEN YEARS CREDIT.
Emigrant homes, with Lodging and Protection for land buyers, provided by Geo. S Harris, Land Commissioner at Burlingtonn, Iowa, and at Lincoln, Nebraska.
For rates of fare to Burlington; Iowa, Lincoln and Omaha; Nebraska, Western States, San Francisco & or any other information, apply to the BURLINGTON AND MISSOURI-RIVER RAILROAD CO.,
16 South Castle Street, Liverpool;
or to their agents:
Newark: W. Hirst, 52, Castle Gate; Gainsboro': W.G. Packer, Church St; Grantham: Hy. Escrit; Worksop: Edwin P. Gilling;
Boston: Chas. Ingalmils'.

This network of agents in Lincolnshire and East Notts. seems firmly established, and members of the clergy appear to have been leading from the front. We cannot know for sure how people from Upton emigrated to America or Canada or Australia, but a report dated July 1883 seems to suggest that the migration was gaining momentum.

'EMIGRATION FROM THE MIDLANDS - More emigrants left the midland counties of England last week than has previously been known for a like period. On Monday last one hundred women and children were dispatched from the New-Street railway

station, Birmingham, for different parts of Australia, and on subsequent days there were large numbers booked for Liverpool en route for Canada and the United States. The station each morning was crowded with emigrants and their friends, and the exciting scenes witnessed and the occasion which gave rise to them have become a general topic of conversation in the district...'

The folk-song "The Leaving of Liverpool" recalls this migration, and mentions a "Yankee packet ship". Some emigrants crossed the Atlantic on these, others on more traditional English sailing ships - square rigged wooden barques which dominated the ocean trades, for these were the last "glorious" days of sail. But there was rarely an easy crossing of the Atlantic, and emigrants were at the mercy of the seas and the winds. By far the best description of such a crossing - from the passengers point of view, at any rate - came from the pen of the giant of English literature best qualified to write it, Charles Dickens, although Nicholas Montserrat was to give a very good idea of the naval officer's experience a hundred year later in "The Cruel Sea". Dickens and his wife sailed from Liverpool to Halifax on January 4th, 1842. He recounted their fifteen days of misery, and that of their fellow passengers, in two long and utterly splendid chapters at the beginning of "American Notes". There is ample scope for two of his formidable arsenal of writing powers - black humour, and the description of untamed violence. Nothing is missed, from the moments when his friends say goodbye to him (as to a man who is going to his execution) to the plight of a wretched steerage passenger on the return trip. Many emigrants were disappointed to find that the streets of New York were not paved with gold, as they had been led to believe, and sold their clothes and belongings to buy return tickets. The steerage passenger in question had no food whatsoever, and was reduced to secretively gnawing the meat bones thrown away by the other people in the steerage. The steam engines on Dicken's sail-assisted paddle-boat, the S.S. Britannia, were so inefficient that the ship started deep in the water, heavily weighed down by the immense tonnage of steam coal that she had to carry. But she survived the continuous storm - just.

'In the gale of last night the life boat had been crushed by one blow of the sea like a walnut shell; and there it hung dangling in the air; a mere faggot of crazy boards. The planking of the paddle-boxes had been torn sheer away. The wheels were exposed and bare; and they whirled and dashed their spray about the decks at random. Chimney, white with crusted salt; topmasts struck; rigging all knotted, tangled, wet and drooping: a gloomier picture it would be hard to look upon.'

Similarly, the first cricket touring party which crossed the Atlantic in 1859 had a rough outward crossing; several of cricketers vowed they would never leave England again. On the return trip the ship encountered severe gales and one of the crew was killed when the sea lifted one of the anchors and crushed him.

The great period of emigration which started in about 1800 and finished in about 1875 saw seven and a half million people cross from Britain and Ireland to lay the foundations of the modern United States and Canada. Even after the opening of the Suez Canal in 1869 the sailing ship was still the most economic carrier of bulky commodities and passengers around the world, but her death knell was ringing in the tunes of the engine makers' hammers in a Scottish shipyard. After 1880 - too late for Dickens and most emigrants - a swifter, more certain method of crossing the Atlantic and the other oceans became available; in 1881 the SS Aberdeen, fitted with triple expansion engines, was launched from Napier's yard in Glasgow. Her steam pressure was

125lbs per square inch, and she reached Melbourne in 42 days. By the end of 1884, with the improvement of boilers, the 150 mark had been reached. In 1887 the 150 pressure mark was passed, and shortly after, the 200 - a pressure per square inch requiring only a fraction more than a pound of coal per horse power per hour. The original low pressure engine had often required more than ten, as on the S.S. Britannia. The final stage in the annihilation of the sailing ship had been reached.

How many emigrants left Upton? No-one can be sure, but it is possible, with the global statistics at one's disposal, to estimate it at about two hundred. What is interesting is that one of them at least was prepared to cross the Atlantic repeatedly. The Charles Foster referred to below was an ancestor of Mary Hall, nee Foster, who lives in the village now, as do her children, Jez Hall and Lizzie Bowes, and her grandchildren. He was born in Upton on September 21st, 1820, and apprenticed to J. Dickenson, miller and baker of Newark.

'(April 1882) - DEATH OF AN UPTON MAN IN AMERICA.... We publish in the usual place in our columns today the death of Mr. Charles Foster, who had been confined to his bed for several weeks with a disease of the liver and rheumatism ... He was thoroughly educated to the profession of music, the piano and organ in particular. In 1850 he came to this city from England, but returning soon after, remaining a few months, and then came back to America, coming directly to this city where he has constantly resided. He has visited England several times since his residence here, and returned from his last visit about three months since. He was widely known, as he has at different times been the organist of several of our most prominent churches ... a quiet, unobtrusive man, but genial and warm in his friendships, and a man of varied study and information. He leaves a wide circle of friends to mourn him. His immediate family is the widow and one daughter, Mrs. L. Morgan.'

Chapter eleven

The End of a Reign

In 1851 there were 117 houses in the village, and only 7 had been uninhabited. The population, excluding the inmates and staff of the workhouse, was 509. There were 132 in the workhouse, of whom about 8 were staff; in 1891 this figure had shrunk to about 100.

The population of Upton continued to decrease, and by 1901, the year of the Queen's death, barely 90 houses were inhabited, and 27 uninhabited. The population had shrunk by about a quarter, to about 380. Many houses still had cesspits with wooden seats above; a good example of a "family four holer" can be seen from Church Meadow Lane, a single story outhouse to the left of Church farm. The four seats were at different heights to suit young and old. There was a sheep dip between the apple trees on the front lawn. The Hall, alone, had electricity; its generator was operated and maintained by Mr.

Alfred Henry Lowe, chauffeur to the Warwicks for twenty-seven years, and it was connected to a row of batteries or accumulators which could store electricity. A bicycling craze was sweeping the land; a bicycle gymkhana was held in Norwood Park; bicycles were advertised in every newspaper; cyclists, male or female, were the butt of every cartoonist. Walter Trueman was so proud of his that he took it into a photographic studio and posed with it, in plus-fours and a check cap. But cycles and leisure clothes were symptomatic of changes; the working classes had found a means of personal mobility other than their legs, and enough money to buy the appropriate outfits.

In 1901 the centre of the village was less open than today. The Green and apple trees were an orchard belonging to the Foster's. The road did not curve but made a sharp angle at the junction with Hockerton Lane, where the Launder's shop stood next to Corner Farm. A terrace of three small brick and pantile houses stood hard against the road immediately opposite Orchard Cottage. A fourth house stood behind them, reached from a drive at the north side of Mayfield House. The white thatched building, a post office and shop until the 1980's, was originally longer; its northern end projected almost to the main road. This was a baker's shop belonging to the Foster family, which sold the bread they had baked in the bakehouse behind, and also flour; the back end was a billiard room. On the other corner of Church Lane stands "The Hollies" also owned by the Fosters, who owned the bakehouse, the single story extension to its east was a grocery shop - the shop door can still be seen in the single story side extension. A fact that throws considerable light on the villagers' claims that Upton was a closely knit village - "everybody knew the name of everybody else's dog" - is that within a hundred yards of the green there were five more rooms, beside the billiard room, which were used for social purposes. The back of the first floor of the "Reindeer" was a long room which was used for dances. It was reached by a flight of steps on the outside of the building which can still be seen. This room was not licensed, but the present occupants have found a trapdoor from the pub below through which beer could be passed. Secondly, at the rear of the bakehouse, where there is now a garden, stood a long wooden shed - The Upton Institute. This was used for socials and whist drives. Thirdly, there was the parish room itself. Fourthly, there was a large room on the first floor at the back of the "French Horn", still in use today for receptions and dinners. Finally, and by invitation only, there was a magnificent ballroom on the ground floor of Upton Hall occupying much of the south-facing front of the house, with a large recessed stage. At the top of Carr Dyke lane can still be seen the village forge, where the Blacksmith Mabbott worked. On the side of the forge facing the road was the village noticeboard; posters were glued up by a man who arrived on a bicycle with a long brush tied to the crossbar, and carrying a bucket. He would attack the village urchins that gathered to jeer with his long-handled brush. The blacksmith lived opposite, on the other side of the lane. Later the forge moved to Home Farm, the home of Olive Key and the late Fred Key. The forge can still be seen, directly opposite Peppers Cottage. There was an awkward step up from the road, which some horses would refuse when taken there to be shod. In that case it was customary to lead them through the gate into the farmyard and in through the small rear door. Young Frederick Trueman lived almost opposite the forge in Rose Cottage; his eldest brother Walter lived in Candant House, with old Fred's widow Elizabeth and his sister Kate. This was the centre of the family building firm. Harry Trueman lived in a Kelham for a while, but after his wife died there in childbirth in 1918 he moved back to Upton and bought High Farm. Ernest, the second oldest, decided that there was not enough work in the village for four builders, and moved to Bleasby.

The fundraising effort of the reign succeeded on September 20th, 1900, when Victoria's life was just four months from its end. One sees that the usual hard-working ladies and musicians were giving the final push to something that had been going on for a long time; a new organ was being installed in the church, and the terms must have been cash, and no credit, as will be deduced by the tones of two reports.

On Thursday last a most successful sale of work was held in the day school in aid of the New Organ Fund. Matters began at 2.30 when the vicar, in introducing Mrs. Becher, made a few preliminary remarks on the object of the sale. The new organ which was in the process of being erected by Messrs, Gray and Davison of London would cost, with incidental expenses, some £170, of which only £115 had been actually subscribed. The vicar expressed his liveliest gratitude to the many friends who had given so generously of their time and means. He hoped that they would be rewarded at the close of the day by the knowledge that success had crowned their efforts ..."

The newer attractions included an air-gun range organised by Guy Warwick, of Upton Hall, and a photographic booth. The very next week the Advertiser announced in another long report that the organ had been dedicated on the 23rd September and gave a long account of the service. A full description of the manuals and pedals was given. Nearly a century later it still gives excellent service, unmodernised, although it was moved to the present position at the back of the church during the second world war from the original position on the south side of the choir, near the Warwicks' private pew. This was a fitting end to the century; a musical instrument which would sound for generations of villagers when the voices of those who had paid for it were long silent. It summed up the attitude of a village which had a hard centre of decent and philanthropic people. The many photographs of the forty or so schoolchildren show them to be well-dressed and disciplined, though not especially cheerful. Their vicar was no longer a lone voice among savages; he had colleagues in nearby parishes who could and would help - a kind of team ministry seems to have existed; there were singers and musicians; concerts, societies, institutes and clubs; but, above all, the village now knew education as an essential, as a necessity for all, rather than as an enviable tool of the rich.

Queen Victoria died. On her accession the village was not much advanced in important respects from Jacobean times; within twenty years of her death two men would fly the Atlantic Ocean in twenty hours. A hundred years later there would still be a cricket club, its traditions maintained and nourished by the families whose names have appeared in these pages, and by executives and accountants rather than clergymen and tailors. Most of their earliest opponents had disappeared and their fields returned to the plough. There are no villagers left who can tell us exactly what life was like at the turn of the century, and we must be grateful for the tantalising glimpses that are handed down to us in oral tradition. One of Harry Trueman's last reminiscences in the 1950's, as he looked ruminatively out at the village street with its tarmac surface and occasional motor vehicle was.

"There aren't as many swallows as there used to be".

"What do you mean?" asked Ron.

"Well, the street used to be covered in horse muck, there were so many horses. There were millions of midges feeding on the horse muck. Hundreds of swallows would fly up and down the street all the summer catching them".

Appendix A
Bibliography

Arlott, John.	Arlott on Cricket.	
Bailey, Trevor.	A History of Cricket.	
Bowes, Bill.	Express Deliveries.	Stanley Paul.
Dickens, Charles.	American Notes.	
Frith, David.	The Fast Men.	Corgi, 1975.
Kilvert, Reverend Francis.	Diaries.	
Lewis, Tony.	Double Century.	Hodder & Stoughton, 1987.

National Census of Great Britain, 1851, 1861, 1871,1881.

Newark Advertiser, 1859-1900.

Punch.

Newark Trade Directory, 1855.

West, Frank.	Rude Forefathers.	Cromwell Press, 1989.
Wisden Cricketer's Almanac,	1987, 1989, 1995.	
Wynne-Thomas, Peter.	An essay; The English Cricketers'trip to Canada and the United States, by Fred Lillywhite.	

Appendix B
Victorian players and officals and years of membership, 1855-1901.

Aldridge, J.	Played 1879.
Beckett.	Played 1887.
Beckett, G.	Played 1900.
Berry, J.	Treasurer, 1859
Bickley, A.H.	Played 1888 (3), 1889. Batsman, bowler.
Breedon, Charles.	1868. Played 1884, 1887 (2). Brickyard Hill, son of bricklayer's labourer.
Brown, J.	Played 1900.
Butler, W.E.	Batsman 1888 (2).
Cobham, J.	Played 1862, 1888 (2), 1891.
Cole, T.	Played 1887.
Collingham, W.	Played 1862.
Cottingham, J.	Played 1887 (3). Bowler.
Cooper, J.	Cooper's cottage. Played 1868.
Cooling, Abraham.	1856-. Played 1879. Greengrocer's son. Singer. Beneficiary of a charity concert, May 25th, 1881, after three long illnesses.
Cullen, E.	Batsman 1868.
Cox, F.	Played 1883.
Cox, J.	1866-. Played 1879, 1880 (2), 1883, 1884, 1887 (3), 1900. Batsman, bowler. Son of farm labourer.
Cox, P.	Played 1900.
Cox, T.	Played 1879-7 (2), 1888 (3), 1889, 1890 (6), 1891 (4), 1900. Bowler.
Cullen, T.	Played 1862.
Curzon, F.	Played 1883.
Curzon, J.	b. 1847. Woodman. Played 1887, bowler.
Curzon, T.	b. 1862. Curzon Cottage. Mother on parish relief. Played 1884, 1887 (2).
Curzon, W.	1838-. Played 1859.
Dayman, H.	Played 1900.
Dixon, W.	Batsman, bowler. 1890 (2).
Dodson, T.	Played 1900.
Doubleday, George.	1844. Farm labourer. Played 1862.
Doubleday, John.	Publican, "The Reindeer". Now "Hallcroft". Steward 1855, played 1859.
Doubleday, Mr.	Played 1868.
Ellis, H.	Played 1900.
Esam, J.	Played 1887, 1888, 1890 (2).
Esam, W.	Batsman, bowler. 1888 (3), 1890.
Fisher, F.	Batsman, opening bowler, 1879, 1880 (2), 1883. Village schooteacher until 1883.
Foster, G.	Played 1862, 1890. Batsman.
Foster, Matthew.	1828-. Tailor. Steward, 1855.

Foster, Robert.	1825-. Baker and grocer. Played 1859.
Foster, Robert Samuel.	b.1855. Baker, The Turnhouse. Opening bat, bowler, 1879-1887 (3), 1888 (4), 1889, 1890.
Foster, T.	Batsman, 1890 (2).
Foster, W.	Played 1888 (2), 1889, batsman.
Gibson, J.	1842-. Farmer. Played 1862.
Gill, Joseph.	1839-. Farmer. Played 1868, 1887, 1888, 1891.
Hallam, J.	Opening bat, opening bowler, 1868.
Hadfield, J.	Opening bat, opening bowler, 1879, 1880.
Hadfield, Thomas.	Played 1887 (4), 1888 (4), 1889. Opening bat, wkt.
Hadfield, W.	Played 1887, bowler.
Halliday, H.G.	b, 1862. School teacher, certificated. Played 1890 (2), 1891 (3).
Hardington, H.	Played 1879.
Hardstaff, B.	Played 1891.
Hatfield, R.	Batsman, opening bowler, 1868.
Hett.	Played 1891
Holmes.	Played 1880.
Hope.	Played 1880.
Horsley, G.	Bowler, 1868.
Jackson, J.	Played 1888.
Johnson, J.	Played 1862.
Keyworth, F.	b. 1848. Joiner. Opening bat, 1879, 1880.
Lawson, J.	Played 1900.
Lee, F.	Played 1888, 1890, batsman.
Lee, J.	Played 1862.
Lidgett, C.	Played 1890 (2).
Lidgett, H.	Played 1890 (2).
Liniker, K.	Played 1890.
Lineker, W.	Played 1887(2).
Linscall.	Played 1883.
Marsh, R.	Played 1900.
Marsh, S.	Played 1900.
Marsh, T.	Played 1900.
Marshall, C.	Played 1859.
Marshall, R.	Played 1888 (4).
Mathers, W.	Batsman, bowler. 1890 (4),1891 (2).
Mills, A.	Played 1890 (4), bowler.
Mills, F.	Played 1883.
Morris, L.	Batsman, 1868.
Neale, F.	Played 1885.
Oldham, W.	Batsman, opening bowler, 1868.
Paling, T.	Played 1868.
Parlby, George.	1835-. Farm labourer. Played 1862, 1868.
Parlby, G.	Played 1900.

Parlby, J.R.	b. 1845. Woodman. Batsman, bowler. 1879-1887 (2), 1888, 1890 (3), 1891 (2). Probably captain.
Parlby, T.	Batsman, 1890 (3), 1891.
Peacocke, Mr. F.O.N.	1864-. Played 1883-1885, 1887 (3). Bowler.
Peacock, W.	Played 1880.
Pollitt, W.	Played 1887 (3), bowler.
Potter, S.	Played 1883. Batsman, bowler.
Pritchett, F.	Played 1900.
Rickett, G.	Boot and shoe maker. Batsman, 1868, 1884.
Randall, G.	Played 1890.
Rawson, E.	Played 1900.
Rawson, H.	Played 1900.
Rawson, J.	Played 1900.
Salt, A.	Batsman, bowler, 1880 (2). Singer.
Savage, H.	Played 1891 (2).
Sharman, H.	Played 1889.
Sheppard, G.	Played 1884, 1900.
Sheppard, Thomas.	1855-. Grocer. Batsman, 1884-1885, 1888, 1891 (3). Blacksmith's son.
Sheppard, William.	1860-. Goods carrier. Played 1880, 1883-1887 (3), 1888 (4), 1889, 1890 (4), 1891 (4), 1900. Bowler, batsman. Blacksmith's son.
Smith, George.	1822-. Farmer and publican. Played 1868.
Suter, T.	Played 1900.
Trueman, Ernest. wkt.	b.1871. Played 1889, 1890 (7), 1891 (4). Batsman
Trueman, Frederick.	1833-1892. Candant House. Bricklayer, three sons. Steward, 1855, played 1859 wk., 1868 opening bowler.
Trueman, Frederick.	1877-1954
Trueman, Henry ("Harry")	1874-1953. Played 1888, 1889, 1890 (7), 1891 (4). Batsman, bowler, professional cricketer, also played for Averham, Mansfield etc.
Trueman, Walter	1868-1951. Played 1887, 1888 (2), 1889, 1890 (7), 1891 (3), 1900. Batsman. Treasurer 1930-1941.
Ulyett, G.	Played 1859, 1862.
Wade.	Opening bat, opening bowler, 1868.
Walker, W.H.	Vicar at Averham. Played 1891 (2).
Warriner.	Batsman, 1868.
Warrener, S.	Played 1884.
Watts, F.	Played 1888.
Watts, W.	Played 1888.
Weightmann, H.	Played 1862.
Whitaker, George.	1833-1899. The Grange. Steward 1855, played 1859.
Whitaker, John.	1837-. The Grange. Played 1859.
Whitaker, Thomas.	1843-. The Grange. Played 1859.
Whitaker, Walter.	1841-. The Grange. Played 1859, 1880, 1885.

Williams, G.	Played 1868.
Willis, F.	Played 1883-1885, batsman. Singer.
Wood, H.	Batsman, bowler. 1890 (2).
Wood, O.	Played 1900.
Woollatt, D.	Played 1891.
Woollatt, J.	b. Leicestershire. Commission agent and grazier. Played 1880 (2), 1885, 1887, 1888, 1900.
Woollatt, T.	Played 1885, 1887.
Woollatt, W.	Batsman, 1887, 1888, 1889, 1890 (4), 1891.
Wright, W.	Played 1880.

<u>Conditions</u>. A batsman is so called if he is placed in the first two, or scores in double figures, or both. A bowler is any man who takes a wicket. The figure in brackets indicateds how many times a player has appeared for the club in that year

---

Appendix C
Matches played against other villages and sides, 1855-1901

Averham, 1859, 1885.
Caunton, 1862.
Farnsfield, 1883.
Fiskerton, 1884 (twice).
F. Parker's XI, Newark, 1888.
Halam, 1887, 1888.
H.W. Walker's XI, 1890.
Kelham, 1887.
Kelham & Averham, 1887 (twice), 1891.
Kirklington, 1890 (twice).

Laxton, 1888,
Maythorne Lace Mills, 1888.
Mr. White's, Nottingham, 1884.
Muskham, 1890 (twice), 1891.
Newark Bulders, 1889.
Newark Castle, 1880.
Newark Hartington, 1880.
Rolleston, 1879.
Winkburn, 1868.

	venue	Result
Monday, 23rd June, 1859		
Averham v. Upton.	Averham.	Won by an innings and nine runs
Thursday, July 31st, 1862.		
Caunton v. Upton.	Caunton.	Abandoned - rain.
Monday, August 3rd, 1868.		
Winkburn v. Upton	Winkburn.	Lost by 74 runs.
Thursday, 17th September, 1868.		
Balderton v. Upton	Balderton.	Won by an innings and six runs.
Tuesday, July 8th, 1879		
Upton v. Rolleston.	Upton.	won by eight wickets.
June 16th, 1880.		
Upton v. Newark Hartington.	Newark	lost by 51 runs.
Wednesday, October 6th, 1880.		
Upton versus Castle CC.	Sconce Hills.	lost by an innings and six runs
Saturday, 18th August, 1883		
Farnsfield (an XI) v. Upton.	Farnsfield.	lost by nine wickets.
Saturday, 19th July, 1884.		
Fiskerton v. Upton (return match)	Upton	lost by six wickets.
Saturday, 27th October, 1884.		
Mr. White's (Nottingham) v. Mr. Parlby's.	Upton.	Won by 16 runs.

Thursday, 9th July, 1885.
    Upton v. Averham.   Upton   lost by five wickets.
Saturday, July 30th, 1887.
    Kelham v. Upton.   Kelham.   lost by 21 runs.
Monday, August 1st, 1887.
    Upton v. Halam.   Upton.   won by 64 runs.
Saturday, September 24th, 1887.
    Upton v. Kelham & Averham.   Kelham.   lost by an innings and 44 runs.

Upton v. Kelham & Averham.
reported on Wednesday, Aug 31st, 1887.   Upton.   won by 24 runs.
Thursday, 5th July, 1888.
    Upton v. Halam.   Upton.   won by 8 wickets.
Saturday, 7th July, 1888.
    Upton v. Maythorne Lace Mills.
        Upton.   won by an innings and 18 runs.
Saturday, July 14th, 1888.
    Upton v. F. Parker's XI (Newark).
        Upton.   won by an innings and 20 runs.
Saturday, July 23rd, 1888.
    Upton v.Laxton.   Laxton.   won by 31 runs.
Saturday, 31st August, 1889.
    Upton v. Newark Builders.   Upton.   won by 24 runs.
Saturday, May 31st, 1890.
    Muskham v. Upton.   Upton.   won by 7 runs.
Saturday. June 21st, 1890.
    Muskham v. Upton   Muskham.   lost by six wickets
Saturday, 26th July, 1890.
    H.W.Walker's xi v. Upton.   Averham.   lost by 10 runs.
reported August 13, 1890 - no date.
    Upton Club(100-7) v. twenty-two (21 all out and 26 for 9).
Saturday 9th August, 1890.
    Kirklington v. Upton.   Kirklington.   Won by 61 runs.
reported August 27, 1890.   Won.
    Upton v. Kirklington.   Upton.   won by 29 runs.
reported October 1st, 1890.
    H. Trueman's team (39) v. W. Trueman's team (27). No result.
(Feast) Thursday, July 9th, 1891.
    Upton C.C.(44) v. Twenty-two(41).   Won
Saturday, 18th July, 1891.
    Averham & Kelham v. Upton.   Kelham.   lost by an innings and 52 runs
Saturday, 15th August, 1891.
    Upton C.C.(87 for 8) v. Twenty-Two(62)   won by 25 runs
        Upton.
Monday, 14th September, 1891.
    Upton v. Muskham.   Muskham.   won by seven wickets.
Saturday, 30th June, 1900.
    Upton C.C. v. Upton Village.   lost by 38 runs.

1859-1901. Played 30, Won 18, Lost 11, Abandoned 1

Appendix D
The First Settlements in Upton, 600-800 AD

It was not within the disciplines of this book to make any attempt at estimating the date of the original settlement of Upton. However, during the research a particular piece of information was found which, though completely baffling to the amateur archaeologist in June 1871, transmits loud and clear signals in 1996, providing that the auditor has some idea of the settlement pattern and, most importantly, the burial practices of the tribes of Angles who first settled the north banks of the Trent Valley. These Angles crossed the North Sea in small or large fleets of long boats at its narrowest known part. They then travelled along the coast in a northerly direction until they found a river - in this case the Humber Estuary, whence they turned south down the Trent. They would have intended to sail past earlier settlements until they found unoccupied land suitable for arable farming, or the rearing of livestock. The ideal site would have water meadows, pasture, moorland and woods to provide timber for building. They would need springs; a bonus would be a river crammed with trout or pike or carp, and a good run of salmon. Ideally, also, they wanted a small hill on which a wooden stockade could be built for defensive purposes; they were very well aware that wherever they went the Vikings could follow.

We may therefore picture longboats full of Anglians, after a long voyage from their native Denmark and its islands, with their horses and cattle lying in the bottom with their feet tied, travelling steadily up the Trent past prosperous villages or fishing villages and farms that had been established since about 600 A.D., past Kelham and Averham and Rolleston. Perhaps wishing that they had made an earlier start themselves, as all the best land had gone already, they would have noticed the mouth of a small river - the Greet, emptying into the Trent at Fiskerton. It is not a particularly wide or deep river, but when we remember that Anglian boats drew only four inches of water, we realise that it would be navigable. There might already have been a settlement or mill where Fiskerton Mill now stands; but pushing or hauling or rowing their boats they would only have had to progress for a couple of miles up the Greet when all the pre-requisites for a succesful settlement appeared where Upton now stands, and they could haul their boats up somewhere near the Racecourse or Upton Mill.

The amateur architect/archaeologiist in 1871 was the Archdeacon Trollope, visiting every church in the Lincoln Dicese, and having his off-the-cuff or learned remarks about each and every one printed in full in the Advertiser. The interesting part of his remarks about Upton are as follows.

'The Archdeacon drew attention to the singular fact, that when the church was last restored some vases were found embedded. Some slight discussion ensued upon this discovery, the archdeacon stating that similar discoveries had been made occasionally in other parts of

England, also in France and Russia. It appears probable that the introduction of these vases was to improve the acoustic properties of the building - that was one theory put forward at any rate'.

The tone of the final part of the last sentence shows that the Advertiser's reporter had learnt to recognise nonsense.

The earliest agreed date for a church on the existing site is 1250, but there have been numerous extensions and rebuildings. During one of these the vases were discovered, presumably deeply embedded among the cut stones and mortar and rammel. It is impossible to imaginge that they served any useful purposes except to fill up space and save the need to cart stone, which is always expensive. So these vases, which presumably were lying close at hand during the rebuilding, were used for that purpose. However, decent vases are useful and difficult to come by, and one cannot imagine the owners surrendering them that easily. So, could the vases have come from any other source?

They could well have been Anglian cremation urns. The Anglians were in the habit of cremating their dead, and then placing the ashes in rather ugly pots, not more than nine inches high. The pots usually had wide mouths and were ornamented with circular patterns and often four or five bumps. They were buried a little way below the surface of the ground near a church.

It seems quite possible that the builders charged with the task of extending the church by building a north aisle had discovered some of these urns while digging the foundations; they were digging in an Anglian burial area. They probably recognised them for what they were, and for reasons connected either with superstition or their religion decided it would be most appropriate to incorporate them within the edifice of the church as near as possible to their original resing place.

When would this have taken place? One relies on Sir Frank Stenton, the historian who wrote the definitive book the Angles and Saxons, and by co-incidence lived in Southwell. He writes that the practice of cremation and internment of the ashes in urns can be dated as early as the 5th century by the associated grave-goods often found. However, the practice became obsolete by the eighth. This would suggest that, if the vases were cremation urns, there must have been a village on the site of Upton, which included a man working as a potter, before the eighth century.

Appendix E

The restoration of the Old Vicarage, by Mrs. Mary Toomey, B.Sc.,J.P. This is quoted verbatim from a letter written to the author on 26th August, 1996.

'All we did was pitch up, pay up (through the nose, having been quite neatly gazumped) and thoroughly enjoy living in Upton for 11 years ... In the spring of 1973 Brian was relocated from Courtaulds in Northern Ireland to Meridian in Nottingham, and after some searching he saw an advertisement in one of the local papers for a private sale of "A Gentleman's Residence of Character" and made an appointment with a Mr. and Mrs. Carr of the Old Vicarage at Upton to view. When he first saw the house it was in a state of considerable renovation i.e. two rooms downstairs had been re-decorated and a cloakroom had been created by hiving off a substantial corner of the kitchen. Presumably this was deemed by the Carrs to be preferable to the downstairs Loo being located in a corridor which sported a window onto the road! The remaining downstairs area was untouched, the kitchen gutted but the window had been enlarged; in the erstwhile scullery the soft water tank in the floor (the contents accessed by a hand-pump at the sink) had been filled in. Upstairs, of the six bedrooms, some had been decorated but one was open to the rafters as Mr. Carr was raising the ceilings and eliminating the attics. Neither of the two bathrooms was connected. To quote Denis Carr "There is 3 weeks work left" - one year later it was still unfinished! All the credit for the renovation must go to him and his wife Jean.

... The Carrs purchased the property at auction in 1972 and paid £6,000 for it. The Reverend Robin Lacey having been offered the Living turned it down on the grounds that the house was uninhabitable, and as a result the Church Commissioners decided to sell it. We bought it in 1973 for an initially agreed price of £30,000 which rose finally to £35,000. That seems an almost modest sum now, but believe me, in 1973 it was considered a huge sum of money (and it felt like it too!) However, we were desperate to "come home" from Northern Island, had seen the house and instantly fallen in love with it and we liked the idea of Southwell and the Minster Grammar School, so we bit on the bullet!

...The Reverend Frank West, Vicar of Upton moved into the Old Vicarage in 1947 as a bachelor. Later, having married, and when his wife was giving birth to their firstborn on a very cold day, the somewhat over enthusiastic efforts to provide sufficient heat for the event, resulted in the floor of the bedroom catching fire. At a later date a Reverend Smith was the vicar and his daughter Barbara ran a school in this same room ... I think that's all I recall about the house, except to say that when Denis Carr had completed all the work he agreed to do, which was sometime in the Autumn of 1974, the house was a constant source of pleasure to our family, and still remains, of the seven houses in which we lived, my very favourite home.'

The reference to a soft water tank is interesting. An advertisement from the "Advertiser" of October 1st, 1873, for a house to let by Mr. Collingham includes

"Hard and soft water". Mary Toomey mentions a soft water tank. All the houses in Church Lane, and possibly throughout the village, prided themselves on having two kinds of water. The hard water tanks in some cases were the cellars, flooded with hard water nearly to the top of the steps. At "The Hollies" it was pumped into the kitchen by means of a cast-iron long-handled pump. The other sources of hard water were the dozens of wells. Soft water was rainwater, collected in an underground tank or in wooden tubs as it came down gutters and pipes from roofs.

Appendix F
A Feat of Strength

There is some doubt about the location of this incident; some witnesses place it on the steps leading to the storeroom on the first floor above the bakehouse in Church Lane, now occupied by Mr. Mike Illsley. The position of these steps may still be seen in the brickwork to the right of the front door. Mr. Burrell himself places the incident at the granary at Springwood farm, which he now farms with his brother, at the junction of Hockerton Lane and the Newark-Mansfield road.

During an autumn in the mid-1950's a group of young men were watching Spen Burrell moving sacks of wheat, weighing 9 stone each, by carrying them on his back. One of these bystanders bet £5 that he could carry a sack up the flight of steps, and that Spen could not. He failed in this task, and Spen's turn came. The sack was put on his back by means on an "icking barrow". Having adjusted it carefully, Spen told his brother John to jump on top of the sack. He then carried both up the flight of steps and won the bet; this was a total weight of nearly thirty stones. Spen was then about eighteen years old. It is reasonable to assume that he was carrying nearly three times his own weight.

To put this into perspective, a trained fireman was expected to carry an inert body equivalent to his own weight - say ten or eleven stones. The maximum weight that a normal man would like to carry for a short distance on the level would be about one hundredweight (eight stone) which is the exact equivalent of a sack of cement.

Some of the bystanders were not particularly surprised by what they saw, for they knew that Spen earnt money during the autumn by helping local farmers with their threshing. He would walk miles to get a day's work. His specialism was to carry the filled sacks of wheat into the granaries. He was paid £1 a day, which rose to 25 shillings in 1960.

Nor was he merely musclebound. At about this time, in company with other young men, he attended a dance in Maplebeck, six miles from Southwell. After the dance had ended, and after they had had plenty to drink, bets were laid as to who could run back to Southwell non-stop. Spen was the only one of the group to achieve this.

Spen was, incidentally, a good fast bowler for the club; a life such as his was the perfect training, and remains so to this day.

The point is that, taken together, these facts give a very good idea of one young man's strength and stamina in the middle of the twentieth century. It is fair to say that the work available to him, and the lack of personal transport, contributed directly to the development of these attributes. This may lead us to a further point; to accept that in the Victorian years the farmworkers of Upton were equally accustomed to such parameters, and that there may well have been many in this mould. To take the point further, there were at least fifteen farms in Upton. We can therefore surmise that generations of strong and fit young men were available to the cricket club.

Appendix G
The "Daddy Upton" photographs.

Mystery surrounds these much printed photographs, for the central figure bearing a yoke and two buckets of water cannot be identified by any modern residents of the village; nor, more significantly, was he known to Harry Trueman. A copy of the photo which includes the flock of sheep hung in High Farm when George Story lodged there as a young farm worker in the nineteen twenties; the identity of "Daddy Upton" was often discussed, but never settled. The 1881 census if of no help; it lists only a Marthia Upton, aged 79, who was a workhouse inmate.

One can attempt a hypothesis. The turn of the century was very much the age of the postcard. Did an enterprising photographer bring the picturesque "Daddy Upton" from another village to add interest to a dull village street scene? The misspelt caption supports this solution. It all seems rather too stilted and posed to be a genuine photograph - why is "Daddy Upton" wearing his Sunday-best clothes? Why is the young lady, also smartly dressed, so amused? Why was he carrying buckets of water around when every house had a well? Who is looking after the sheep? Of more certain interest is the white gabled outhouse to the left of the road. This is where Walter Trueman kept his building tools, and it was cleaned out and whitewashed every spring, as the photograph suggests.

The second photograph, showing Warriner's Cottage and Hockerton Lane in the early twentieth century, is much more authentic. The dray is from Caudwell's Mill, in Southwell, and is loaded with sacks of wheat. The lady to the right is Mrs. Jane Launders, who owned the post office and shop to the right of the picture. She would smoke a pipe in her parlour in secrecy; she had a soft spot for George Story, and would sell him "Five Woodbines" long before he should have been smoking. Jane would push a handcart to Spring Wood on the Mansfield road to gather firewood; on the return trip it was too heavy for her, so George would push the cart, and be rewarded with a packet of black and white humbugs when they arrived back at the shop. The lady in the centre of the group is Miss Lawson, who was the postmistress.